Doris Lessing was born of British parents in Persia in 1919 and was taken to South Africa when she was five. She spent her childhood on a large farm in Southern Rhodesia and first came to England in 1949. She brought with her the manuscript of her first novel, *The Grass Is Singing*, which was published in 1950 with outstanding success in Britain, in America and in ten European countries. Since then her international reputation not only as a novelist, but as a non-fiction and short-story writer has flourished. For her collection of short novels, *Five*, she was honoured with the Somerset Maugham Award. Among her other celebrated novels are the five-volume *Children of Violence* series, *The Golden Notebook*, *The Summer Before the Dark*, *The Memoirs of a Survivor*. Many of her short stories have been collected in two volumes entitled *To Room Nineteen* and *The Temptation of Jack Orkney*; while her African stories appear in *This Was the Old Chief's Country* and *The Sun Between Their Feet*.

Shikasta, the first in the series of novels with the overall title of CANOPUS IN ARGOS: ARCHIVES, was published in 1979; the second, *The Marriages Between Zones Three, Four, and Five*, in 1980 and the third, *The Sirian Experiments*, in 1981, when it was short-listed for the Booker McConnell Prize.

By the same author

NOVELS
The Grass Is Singing
The Golden Notebook
Briefing for a Descent into Hell
Memoirs of a Survivor
The Summer Before the Dark

In the novel-sequence 'Children of Violence'
Martha Quest
A Proper Marriage
A Ripple from the Storm
Landlocked
The Four-Gated City

'Canopus in Argos: Archives'
Shikasta
The Marriages Between Zones Three, Four, and Five
The Sirian Experiments

NON-FICTION
In Pursuit of the English
Going Home

SHORT STORIES
Five
The Habit of Loving
A Man and Two Women
The Story of a Non-Marrying Man and Other Stories
Winter in July
The Black Madonna
This Was the Old Chief's Country (Collected African Stories, Vol. 1)
The Sun Between Their Feet (Collected African Stories, Vol. 2)
To Room Nineteen (Collected Stories, Vol. 1)
The Temptation of Jack Orkney (Collected Stories, Vol. 2)

PLAYS
Play with a Tiger

Doris Lessing

Particularly Cats

A PANTHER BOOK

GRANADA
London Toronto Sydney New York

Published by Granada Publishing Limited in 1979
Reprinted in 1980, 1981

ISBN 0 586 04699 2

First published in Great Britain by
Michael Joseph Ltd 1967
Copyright © Doris Lessing Productions Ltd 1967

Granada Publishing Limited
Frogmore, St Albans, Herts AL2 2NF
and
36 Golden Square, London W1R 4AH
866 United Nations Plaza, New York, NY 10017, USA
117 York Street, Sydney, NSW 2000, Australia
100 Skyway Avenue, Rexdale, Ontario, M9W 3A6, Canada
61 Beach Road, Auckland, New Zealand

Set, printed and bound in Great Britain by
Cox & Wyman Ltd, Reading
Set in Intertype Plantin

TO MY DAUGHTER, JEAN WISDOM,
WHO ENJOYS LIVING WITH CATS

CHAPTER ONE

The house being on a hill, hawks, eagles, birds of prey
that lay spiralling on air currents over the bush were
often at eye level, sometimes below it. You'd look down
on sun-glistening brown and black wings, a six-foot
spread of them, tilting as the bird banked on a curve.
Down in the fields, you could lie very still in a furrow,
preferably where the plough had bitten deep as it turned,
under a screen of grass and leaves. Legs, too pale against
reddish-brown soil in spite of sunburn, had to be scattered with earth, or dug into it. Hundreds of feet up,
a dozen birds circled, all eyeing the field for small movement of mouse, birds, or mole. You would choose one,
straight overhead perhaps; perhaps for a moment fancy
an exchanged glance eye to eye: the cold staring eye of
the bird into coldly curious human eye. Under the
narrow bulletlike body betwen great poised wings the
claws were held ready. After a half a minute, or twenty,
the bird plummeted straight on to the tiny creature it
had chosen; then up and away it went in a wide steady
beat of wings, leaving behind an eddy of red dust and
a hot rank smell. The sky was as it had been: a tall blue
silent space with its scattered groups of wheeling birds.
But up on the hill a hawk might easily zoom in sideways
from the air circuit where it had been lying to choose its
prey – one of our chickens. Or even fly uphill along
one of the roads through the bush, the great spread of
wings held cautious against overhang of branch: bird
acting, surely, against its nature in speeding thus along
an air avenue through trees rather than dropping
through air to earth?

Our chickens were, or at least that is how their enemies saw it, an always renewed supply of meat for the hawks, owls, and wild cats for miles around. From sunup till sundown, fowls moved over the exposed crown of the hill, marked for marauders by gleaming black, brown, white feathers, and a continuous clucking, crowing, scratching and strutting.

On the farms in Africa it is the custom to cut the tops off paraffin and petrol tins and fix glistening squares of metal to flash in the sun. To scare the birds off, it is said. But I've seen a hawk come in from a tree to take a fat drowsy hen off her hatching eggs, and that with dogs, cats, and people, black and white, all around her. And once, sitting at a domestic spread of tea outside the house, a dozen people were witness to a half-grown kitten being snatched from the shade under a bush by a swooping hawk. During the long hot silence of midday, the sudden squawking or crowing or flustering of feathers might as often mean that a hawk had taken a fowl as that a cock had trod a hen. There were plenty of chickens though. And so many hawks there was no point in shooting them. At any moment, standing on the hill looking at the sky, there was certain to be a circling bird within half a mile. A couple of hundred feet below it, a tiny patch of shadow flitted over trees, over fields. Sitting quiet under a tree I've seen creatures freeze, or go to cover when the warning shadow from great wings far above touched them, or darkened momentarily the light on grass, leaves. There was never only one bird. Two, three, four birds circled in a bunch. Why just there, you'd wonder? Of course! They were all working, at different levels, the same air spiral. A bit further off, another group. Careful looking – and the sky was full of black specks; or, if the sunlight caught them just so, shining specks, like motes in a shaft of light from a window. In all those miles of blue air, how many hawks? Hundreds? And every one of them able to make the journey to our fowl flock in a few minutes.

So the hawks were not shot. Unless in rage. I remember, when that kitten vanished mewing into the sky in the hawk's claws, my mother exploded the shotgun after it. Futilely of course.

If the day hours were for hawks, dawn and dusk were for owls. The chickens were shooed into their runs as the sun went down, but the owls sat in their hour on the trees; and a late sleepy owl might take a bird in the very early sunlight as the runs were opened.

Hawks for sunlight; owls for half-light; but for the night, cats, wild cats.

And here there was some point in using a gun. Birds were free to move over thousands of miles of sky. A cat had a lair, a mate, kittens – at least a lair. When one chose our hill to live on, we shot it. Cats came at night to the fowl-runs, found impossibly small gaps in walls or wire. Wild cats mated with our cats, lured peaceful domestic pussies off to dangerous lives in the bush for which, we were convinced, they were not fitted. Wild cats brought into dubious question the status of our comfortable beasts.

One day the black man who worked in the kitchen said he had seen a wild cat in a tree halfway down the hill. My brother was not there; so I took the .22 rifle and went after it. It was high midday: not the time for wild cats. On a half-grown tree, the cat was stretched along a branch, spitting. Its green eyes glared. Wild cats are not pretty creatures. They have ugly yellowy-brown fur, which is rough. And they smell bad. This cat had taken a chicken in the last twelve hours. The earth under the tree was scattered with white feathers and bits of meat that already stank. We hated wild cats, which spat and clawed and hissed and hated us. This was a wild cat. I shot it. It slumped off the branch to my feet,

9

writhed a little among blowing white feathers, and lay still. Usually I would have picked up that carcass by its mangy smelly tail and dropped it into a nearby disused well. But something bothered me about this cat. I bent to look at it. The shape of its head was wrong for a wild cat; and the fur, rough as it was, was too soft for wild-cat fur. I had to admit it. This was no wild cat, it was one of ours. We recognized it, that ugly corpse, as Minnie, an enchanting pet from two years before who had disappeared – taken, we thought, by a hawk or an owl. Minnie had been half Persian, a soft caressing creature. This was she, the chicken-eater. And, not far from the tree where she was shot, we found a litter of wild kittens; but these were really wild, and human beings were their enemies: our legs and arms were bitten and scratched in proof of it. So we destroyed them. Or rather, my mother saw that they were destroyed; because some law of the household I did not until much later reflect about made this sort of nasty work hers.

If you think about it a little: there were always cats at the house. No vet nearer than Salisbury, seventy miles off. No 'doctoring' of cats that I can remember, certainly not of female cats. Cats mean kittens, plentiful and frequent. Someone had to get rid of unwanted kittens. Perhaps the Africans who worked in the house and kitchen? I can remember how often the words *bulala yena* sounded. (Kill it!) The wounded and weakly animals and birds of the house and farm: *bulala yena!*

But there was a shotgun in the house, and a revolver, and it was my mother who used them.

Snakes, for instance, were usually dealt with by her. We always had snakes. This sounds dramatic, and I suppose it was; but they were something we lived with. I was not nearly as afraid of them as I was of spiders – enormous, various and innumerable, that made my life a misery. There were cobras, black mambas, puff-adders and night-adders. And a particularly nasty one called a boomslang whose habit it is to coil around a branch, a verandah post, something off the ground, and spit into the faces of those disturbing it. It is often somewhere at eye-level, so people get blinded. But through twenty years of snakes, the only bad thing that happened was when a boomslang spat into my brother's eyes. His sight was saved by an African who used bush medicine.

But alarms were always being sounded. There's a snake in the kitchen; or on the verandah; or in the dining-room; everywhere, it seemed. Once I nearly picked a night-adder up, mistaking it for a skein of darning wool. But it feared me first, and its hissing saved us both: I ran; and it got away. Once a snake got into the writing desk which was a nest of paper-stacked pigeon-holes. It took my mother and the servants hours to frighten the creature out so that she could shoot it. Once a snake, a mamba, got under the grain bin in the store hut. She had to lie on her side and shoot the thing from a foot away.

A snake in the woodpile raised an alarm; and I caused the death of a favourite cat by saying I had seen the snake creeping in between two logs. What I had seen was the cat's tail. My mother shot at something greyish that moved; and out shrieked the cat, its side blown out, all red and raw. It thrashed and yelled among the wood chips, its small bleeding heart showing between fragile broken ribs. It died, while my mother wept and petted it. Meanwhile the cobra was looped around a high log a couple of yards away.

Once a great tumult of shouts and warnings; and there, on a rocky path between hibiscus bushes and Christ's-thorn, was a cat in combat with a slim dark dancing snake. The snake crept into the yard-wide thorn hedge and stayed there, glittering its eyes at the cat, who could not get near it. The cat stayed there all afternoon, walking around the thorny mass which held the snake, spitting at it, hissing at it, miaowing. But when the dark came, the snake crept away, unharmed.

Flashes of memory, stories without beginnings or ends. What happened to the cat who lay stretched out on my mother's bed, miaowing with pain, its eyes swollen up from a spitting snake? Or the cat who came crying into the house, her belly dragging to the ground with unused milk? We went to see to her kittens in the old box in the tool-shed, but they were gone; and the servant examined marks in the dust around the box and said, '*Nyoka*'. A snake.

In childhood, people, animals, events appear, are accepted, vanish, with no explanation offered or asked for.

But now, remembering cats, always cats, a hundred incidents involving cats, years and years of cats, I am astounded at the hard work they must have meant. In London now I have two cats; and often enough I say, What nonsense that one should have all this trouble and worry on account of two small animals.

All that work would have been done by my mother. Farm work for the man; housework for the woman, even if the house did involve so very much more work than one associates with housework in a town. It was her work, too, because a nature claims the labour that goes with it. She was humane, sensible, shrewd. She was above all, and in every detail, practical. But more than that: she was one of that part of humankind *which understands how things work;* and works with them. A grim enough role.

My father understood well enough; he was a countryman. But his attitude came out as protest; when something had to be done, steps had to be taken, a final stand was being made – and my mother was making it. 'So that's that! I suppose!' he'd say, in ironic anger which was also admiring. 'Nature,' he'd say, capitulating, 'is all very well, if it's kept in its place.'

But my mother, nature her element, indeed her duty and her burden, did not waste time on sentimental philosophy. 'It's all very well for you, isn't it?' she'd say; humorous, humorous if it killed her; but resentful of course, for it was not my father who drowned the kittens, shot the snake, killed the diseased fowl, or burned sulphur in the white ant nest: my father liked white ants, enjoyed watching them.

Which makes it even harder to understand what led to the frightful weekend when I was left alone with my father and about forty cats.

All I can remember from that time in the way of explanation is the remark: 'She's got soft-hearted and can't bear to drown a kitten.'

It was said with impatience, with irritation and – from me – cold hard anger. At that time I was in combat with my mother, a fight to the death, a fight for survival, and perhaps that had something to do with it, I don't know. But I now wonder, appalled, what sort of breakdown in her courage had taken place. Or perhaps it was a protest? What inner miseries expressed themselves so? What was she in fact saying during that year when she would not drown kittens, or have put to death the cats who badly needed it? And, finally, why did she go away and leave us two, knowing perfectly well, because she must have known, since it was loudly and frequently threatened, what was going to happen?

A year, less, of my mother's refusal to act her role as regulator, arbiter, balance between sense and the senseless proliferations of nature, had resulted in the house, the sheds around the house, the bush that surrounded the farmstead, being infested by cats. Cats of all ages; cats tame and wild and the stages in between; cats mangy and sore-eyed and maimed and crippled. Worse, there were half a dozen cats in kitten. There was nothing to prevent us, within a few weeks, from becoming the battleground for a hundred cats.

Something had to be done. My father said it. I said it. The servants said it. My mother tightened her lips, said nothing, but went away. Before she left she said goodbye to her favourite puss, an old tabby who was the mother of them all. She stroked her gently, and cried. That I do remember, my feeling of futility because I could not understand the helplessness of those tears.

The moment she had gone, my father said several times, 'Well, it's got to be done, hasn't it?' Yes, it had; and so he rang up the vet in town. Not at all a simple business this. The telephone was on a line shared by twenty other farmers. One had to wait until the gossiping and the farm news had fallen silent; then ring up the station; then ask for a line to town. They called back when there was a line free. It might take an hour, two hours. It made it much worse, having to wait, watching the cats, wishing the ugly business over. We sat, side by side on the table in the dining-room, waiting for the telephone to give our particular ring. At last we got the vet, who said the least cruel way to kill grown cats was to chloroform them. There was no chemist's shop nearer than Sinoia, twenty miles off. We drove to Sinoia, but the chemist's shop was shut for the weekend. From Sinoia we rang Salisbury and asked a chemist to put a large bottle of chloroform on to the train next day. He said he would try. That night we sat out in front of the house under the stars; which is where our evenings were spent unless it rained. We were miserable, angry, guilty. We went to bed very early to make the time pass. Next day was Saturday. We drove to the station, but the chloroform was not on the train. On Sunday a cat gave birth to six kittens. They were all deformed: there was something wrong with each of them. Inbreeding, my father said it was. If so, it is a remarkable thing that less than a year of it could transform a few healthy animals into an army of ragged sick cripples. The servant disposed of the new kittens, and we spent another miserable day. On Monday we drove to the station, met the train, and came back with the chloroform. My mother was to come back on Monday night. We got a large airtight biscuit tin, put an old sad sick cat into it, with a tampon soaked in chloroform. I do not recommend this method. The vet said it would be instantaneous; but it was not.

In the end, the cats were rounded up and put into a room. My father went into the room with his First World War revolver, more reliable, he said, than a shotgun. The gun sounded again, again, again, again. The cats that were still uncaught had sensed their fate and were raging and screaming all over the bush, with people after them. My father came out of the room at one point, very white, with tight angry lips and wet eyes. He was sick. Then he swore a good deal, then he went back into the room and the shooting continued. At last he came out. The servants went in and carried off the corpses to the disused well.

Some of the cats had escaped – three never came back at all to the murderous household, so they must have gone wild and taken their chances. When my mother returned from her trip, and the neighbour who had brought her had gone, she walked quiet and uncommenting through the house where there was now one cat, her old favourite, asleep on her bed. My mother had not asked for this cat to be spared, because it was old, and not very well. But she was looking for it; and she sat a long time stroking and talking to it. Then she came out to the verandah. There sat my father and there I sat, murderers, and feeling it. She sat down. He was rolling a cigarette. His hands were still shaking. He looked up at her and said: 'That must never happen again.'

And I suppose it never did.

CHAPTER TWO

I was angry over the holocaust of cats, because of its preventable necessity; but I don't remember grieving. I was insulated against that because of my anguish over the death of a cat some years before, when I was eleven. I said then over the cold heavy body that was, inexplicably, the feathery-light creature of yesterday: Never again. But I had sworn that before, and I knew it. When I was three, my parents said, I was out for a walk with the nurse, in Tehran, and in spite of her protests, had picked up a starving kitten from the street and come home with it. This was my kitten, they said I said, and I fought for it when the household refused to give it shelter. They washed it in permanganate because it was filthy; and thereafter it slept on my bed. I would not let it be taken away from me. But of course it must have been, for the family left Persia, and the cat stayed behind. Or perhaps it died. Perhaps – but how do I know? Anyway, somewhere back there, a very small girl had fought for and won a cat who kept her days and nights company; and then she lost it.

After a certain age – and for some of us that can be very young – there are no new people, beasts, dreams, faces, events: it has all happened before, they have appeared before, masked differently, wearing different clothes, another nationality, another colour; but the same, the same, and everything is an echo and a repetition; and there is no grief even that it is not a recurrence of something long out of memory that expresses itself in unbelievable anguish, days of tears, loneliness, knowledge of betrayal – and all for a small, thin, dying cat.

17

I was sick that winter. It was inconvenient because my big room was due to be whitewashed. I was put in the little room at the end of the house. The house, nearly but not quite on the crown of the hill, always seemed as if it might slide off into the maize fields below. This tiny room, not more than a slice off the end of the house, had a door, always open, and windows, always open, in spite of the windy cold of a July whose skies were an interminable light clear blue. The sky, full of sunshine; the fields, sunlit. But cold, very cold. The cat, a bluish-grey Persian, arrived purring on my bed, and settled down to share my sickness, my food, my pillow, my sleep. When I woke in the mornings, my face turned to half-frozen linen; the outside of the fur blanket on the bed was cold; the smell of fresh whitewash from next door was cold and antiseptic; the wind lifting and laying the dust outside the door was cold – but in the crook of my arm, a light purring warmth, the cat, my friend.

At the back of the house a wooden tub was let into the earth, outside the bathroom, to catch the bathwater. No pipes carrying water to taps on that farm: water was fetched by ox-drawn cart when it was needed, from the well a couple of miles off. Through the months of the dry season the only water for the garden was the dirty bathwater. The cat fell into this tub when it was full of hot water. She screamed, was pulled out into a chill wind, washed in permanganate, for the tub was filthy and held leaves and dust as well as soapy water, was dried, and put into my bed to warm. But she sneezed and wheezed and then grew burning hot with fever. She had pneumonia. We dosed her with what there was in the house, but that was before antibiotics, and so she died. For a week she lay in my arms purring, purring, in a rough trembling hoarse little voice that became weaker, then was silent; licked my hand; opened enormous green eyes when I called her name and besought her to live; closed them, died, and was thrown into the deep shaft – over a hundred feet deep it was – which had gone dry, because the underground water streams had changed their course one year and left what we had believed was a reliable well a dry, cracked, rocky shaft that was soon half filled with rubbish, tin cans and corpses.

That was it. Never again. And for years I matched cats in friends' houses, cats in shops, cats on farms, cats in the street, cats on walls, cats in memory, with that gentle blue-grey purring creature which for me was the cat, the Cat, never to be replaced.

And besides, for some years my life did not include extras, unnecessaries, adornments. Cats had no place in an existence spent always moving from place to place, room to room. A cat needs a place as much as it needs a person to make its own.

And so it was not till twenty-five years later that my life had room for a cat.

CHAPTER THREE

That was in a large ugly flat in Earls Court. What was needed, we decided, was a tough uncomplicated undemanding cat able to fend for itself in what was clearly, and at any glance from the rear windows, a savage battle for power along the walls and back yards. It should catch mice and rats and otherwise eat what was put before it. It should not be purebred and therefore delicate.

This formula had of course nothing to do with London, it related to Africa. For instance, on the farm we fed cats bowls of warm milk as the pails came up from the milking; favourites got scraps from the table; but they never got meat – they caught their own. If they got sick, and had not recovered in a few days, they were destroyed. And on a farm you can keep a dozen cats without thought of a dirt box. As for the battles and balances of power, they were fought and defended over a cushion, a chair, a box in the corner of a shed, a tree, a patch of shade. They carved out territories for themselves against each other, wild cats, and the farm dogs. A farmhouse is open terrain and therefore there is much more fighting than in a city, where a cat, a couple of cats, will own a house or a flat and defend these against visitors or assailants. What these two cats will do to each other inside the boundary line is another matter. But the defence line against aliens is the back door. A friend of mine once had to put a dirt box inside the house for weeks, in London, because her tomcat was in a state of siege from a dozen others who sat all around the walls and trees of the garden, waiting for a kill. Then the tides of war flowed differently, and he was able to claim his own garden again.

My cat was a half-grown black-and-white female of undistinguished origin, guaranteed to be clean and amenable. She was a nice enough beast, but I did not love her; never succumbed; was, in short, protecting myself. I thought her neurotic, overanxious, fussy; but that was unfair, because a town cat's life is so unnatural that it never learns the independence a farm cat has. I was bothered because she waited for people to come home – like a dog; must be in the same room and be paid attention – like a dog; must have human attendance when she had kittens. As for her food habits, she won that battle in the first week. She never, not once, ate anything but lightly cooked calves' liver, and lightly boiled whiting. Where did she get these tastes? I demanded of her ex-owner, who of course did not know. I put down tinned food for her, and scraps from the table; but it wasn't until we were eating liver that she showed interest. Liver it was to be. And she would not eat liver cooked in anything but butter. Once I decided to starve her into submission. 'Ridiculous that a cat should be fed, etc., etc., when people in other parts of the world are starving, etc.' For five days I put down cat food, put down table scraps. For five days she looked critically at the plate, and walked off. I would take up the stale food every evening, open a new tin, refill her milk bowl. She sauntered over, inspected what I had provided, took a little milk, strolled away. She got thinner. She must have been very hungry. But in the end it was I who cracked.

At the back of that big house a wooden stairway led down from the first-floor landing to the yard. There she sat, able to survey half a dozen yards, the street, a shed. When she first arrived, cats came from all around to examine the newcomer. She sat on the top step, able to fly indoors if they came too close. She was half the size of the big waiting tomcats. Much too young, I thought, to get pregnant; but before she was fully grown she was pregnant, and it did her no good to have kittens when she was still one herself.

Which brings me to – our old friend nature. Which is supposed to know so well. In a state of nature, does a she-cat become pregnant before she is fully grown? Does she have kittens four, five times a year, six to a litter? Of course, a cat is not only an eater of mice and birds; she is also provider of food for the hawks that lie in the air over the trees where she is hidden with her kittens. A baby kitten, strolling out from shelter in its first curiosity, will vanish into the claws of a hawk. Very likely a she-cat occupied with catching food for herself and her kittens will be able to protect only one kitten, perhaps two. It is noticeable that a tame cat, if she has six, five kittens, and you take two away, will hardly notice: she'll complain, look for them briefly, and then it is forgotten. But if she has two kittens, and one disappears before its proper time for going, after six weeks, then she is in a frenzy of anxiety and will look for it all over the house. A litter of six kittens in a warm basket in a town house can be seen, perhaps, as eagle and hawk fodder in the wrong place? But then, how inflexible is nature, how unpliable: if cats have been the friends of man for so many centuries, could nature not have adapted itself, just a little, away from the formula: five or six kittens to a litter, four times a year?

This cat's first litter was heralded by much complaint. She knew something was going to happen; and was making sure somebody would be around when it did. On the farm, cats went off to have kittens in some well-hidden and dark place; and they reappeared a month later with their brood to introduce them to the milk bowls. I can't remember having to provide one of our farm cats with a littering place. The black-and-white cat was offered baskets, cupboards, the bottoms of wardrobes. She did not seem to like any of them, but followed us around for two days before the birth, rubbing up against our legs and miaowing. When she started labour, it was on the kitchen floor, and that was because people were in the kitchen. A cold blue linoleum, and on it, a fat cat, miaowing for attention, purring anxiously, watching her attendants in case they left her. We brought in a basket, put her in it and left to do some work. She followed. So it was clear we must stay with her. She laboured for hours and hours. At last the first kitten appeared, but it was the wrong way. One person held the cat, another pulled the slippery back legs of the kitten. It came out, but the head got stuck. The cat bit and scratched and yelled. A contraction expelled the kitten, and at once the half-demented cat turned around and bit the kitten at the back of its neck and it died. When the other four kittens were safely born, the dead one proved to be the biggest and strongest. That cat had six litters, and each litter had five kittens, and she killed the first-born kitten in each litter, because she had such pain with it. Apart from this, she was a good mother.

The father was a very large black cat with whom, when she was on heat, she went rolling around the yard; and who, otherwise, would sit on the bottom step of the wooden flight licking his fur, while she sat on the top step licking hers. She did not like him coming into the flat – chased him out. When the kittens were at the stage that they could find their way down to the yard, they sat on the steps, one, two, three, four, all mixtures of black and white, and looked in fear at the big watchful tom. The mother, finally, would go first, tail erect, ignoring the black cat. The kittens went after her, past him. In the yard she taught them cleanliness while he watched. Then she came first up the steps; and they came after, one, two, three, four.

They would eat nothing but lightly cooked liver, and lightly boiled whiting; which fact I concealed from their potential owners.

Mice were only objects of interest to that cat, and to all her kittens.

The flat had a contrivance I've not seen in any other London place. Someone had taken a dozen bricks out of the kitchen wall, put a metal grille on the outside, and a door on the inside; so there was a sort of food safe in the wall, unsanitary if you like, but it filled the place of that obsolete necessity, a larder. There bread and cheese could be kept in the proper cool but unrefrigerated conditions where they remained moist. To this baby larder, however, came mice. They lived in the walls, and had been conditioned away from any but the most vestigial fear of humans. If I came suddenly into the kitchen and found a mouse, it would look at me, bright-eyed, and wait for me to go. If I stayed and kept quiet, it ignored me, and went on looking for food. If I made a loud noise or threw something at it, it slipped into the wall, but without panic.

I was unable to bring myself to put down a steel trap for these confiding creatures; I felt, however, that a cat was, so to speak, playing fair. But the cat had taken no notice of the mice. One day I came into the kitchen and saw the cat lying on the kitchen table, watching two mice on the floor.

Perhaps the presence of kittens would prompt her supposedly real instincts? Soon she gave birth, and when the kittens were old enough to come downstairs, I put the cat and four kittens into the kitchen, withdrew solid food, and locked them all in for the night. I came down towards dawn for a glass of water, switched the light on, and saw the cat stretched out on the floor, feeding the kittens, one, two, three, four; while a couple of feet away a mouse sat up, disturbed by the light, but not by the cat. The mouse did not even run away, but waited for me to leave.

The cat enjoyed, or tolerated, the company of mice; and disarmed a rather silly dog from downstairs who, on the point of chasing her, capitulated because she, apparently not knowing that dogs were enemies, wound herself around his legs, purring. He became her friend, and the friend of all her kittens. But she did show terror on an occasion when, if cats are creatures of the night, on terms with the dark, she should have remained calm.

One afternoon, night descended on London. I stood at the kitchen window, drinking an after-lunch coffee with a visitor, when the air got dark and dirty, and the street lights came on. From full daylight to full heavy dark took ten minutes, less. We were frightened. Had our sense of time gone? Had that bomb finally exploded somewhere and covered our earth with a filthy cloud? Had one of those death factories with which this pretty island is dotted accidentally let off a lethal gas? Were these, in short, our last moments? No information, so we stood at the window and watched. It was a heavy, breathless, sulphurous sky; a yellow-blackish dark; and the air burned our throats, as it does in a mine shaft after an explosion.

It was extraordinarily silent. In moments of crisis, this waiting quiet is London's first symptom, more disturbing than any other.

Meanwhile the cat sat on the table, trembling. From time to time she let out – not a miaow, but a wail, an interrogative plaint. Lifted off the table and petted, she struggled, jumped down, then crept, not fled, up the stairs, and got under a bed, where she lay shivering. Just like a dog, in fact.

Half an hour later, the dark lifted out of the sky. A contradictory pattern of wind currents had trapped the filthy exhalations from the city which are normally dispelled upwards, under a ceiling of obdurately motionless air. Then a new wind blew, shifted the mass, and the city breathed again.

The cat stayed under the bed all afternoon. When she was finally coaxed down, in a clear fresh evening light, she sat on the windowsill and watched the dark fall — the real dark. Then she licked and repaired her rough and frightened fur, drank some milk, became herself.

Just before I left that flat, I had to go away for a weekend, and a friend cared for the cat. When I came back, she was in the hands of a vet, with a broken pelvis. The house had a flat roof outside a high window, where she used to sit sunning herself. For some reason she fell off this roof, which was three storeys up, into an areaway. She must have had a bad fright of some kind. Anyway, she had to be killed and I decided to keep cats in London was a mistake.

The next place I lived in was impossible for cats. It was a block of six tiny flats, one above another along a cold stone staircase. No yard or garden: the nearest exposed earth was probably in Regent's Park, half a mile away. Country unsuitable for cats, you'd think; but a large yellow tortoiseshell cat decorated a corner grocer's window; and he said the cat slept there alone at night; and when he went on holiday he turned it out into the street to fend for itself. It was no use remonstrating with him, because he asked: Did it look well and happy? Yes, it did. And it had been living like this for five years.

For a few months a large black cat lived on the staircase of the flats, belonging, apparently, to nobody. It wanted to belong to one of us. It would sit waiting until a door opened to let someone in or out, and then miaow, but tentatively, like one who has had many rebuffs. It drank some milk, ate some scraps, weaved around legs, asking to be allowed to stay. But without insistence, or, indeed, hope. No one asked it to stay. There was the question, as always, of cat's dirt. No one could face running up and down those stairs with smelly boxes to and from the rubbish bins. And besides, the owner of the flats wouldn't like it. And besides, we tried to comfort ourselves, it probably belonged to one of the shops and was visiting. So it was fed only.

In the daytime it sat on the pavement, watching the traffic, or wandered in and out of the shops: an urbane old cat; a gentle cat; a cat without pretensions.

At the corner was a site where three fruit and vegetable barrows stood, owned by three old people: two brothers, a fat brother and a thin brother, and the wife of the fat one, who was also fat. They were tiny people, five foot high, and always making jokes and always about the weather. When the cat visited them it sat under a barrow and ate bits from their sandwiches. The little round lady, who had red cheeks, so red they were blackish, and who was married to the little round brother, said she would take the cat home with her, but she was afraid her own Tibby wouldn't be at all pleased. The little thin brother, who had never married and who lived with them, joked that he could take it home for company, and defend it against Tibby: a man who had no wife needed a cat. I think he would have done; but he died suddenly of heat stroke. Whatever the temperature, those three people were wrapped up in every kind of scarf, jacket, jersey, coat. The thin brother wore, invariably, an overcoat over a bundle of clothes. If the temperature went above fifty-five, he complained it was a heat wave, and he felt the heat terribly. I suggested he wouldn't be so hot if he didn't wear so many clothes. But this was an attitude towards clothes that was clearly foreign to him: it made him uneasy. One year we had

27

a long spell of fine weather, a real London heat wave. Every day I descended to a street which was gay, warm, friendly with people in summer clothes. But the little old people still wore their head scarves and their neck scarves and their jerseys. The old lady's cheeks grew redder and redder. They joked all the time about the heat. In the shade at their feet under the barrow, the cat lay stretched among fallen plums and bits of wilting lettuce. Towards the end of the second week of the heat wave, the bachelor brother died of a stroke and that was the end of the cat's chance of a home.

For a few weeks he had luck, and was welcome in the pub. This was because Lucy, the prostitute who lived in the ground-floor flat of our building, used that pub in the evenings. She took him in with her, and sat on a high stool in a corner by the bar, with the cat on a stool beside her. She was an amiable lady, much liked in the pub; and anybody she chose to take in with her was made welcome too. When I went in to buy cigarettes or a bottle, there sat Lucy and the cat. Her admirers, many and from all parts of the world, old customers and new, and of all ages, were buying her drinks and coaxing the barman and his wife to give the cat milk and potato crisps. But the novelty of a cat in a bar must have worn off, because soon Lucy was working the bar without the cat.

When the cold weather and the nights of early dark came, the cat was always well up the staircase before the great doors were closed. It slept in as much of a warm corner as it could find on that inhuman uncarpeted stretch of stone steps. When it was very cold, one or other of us would ask the cat in for the night; and in the morning it thanked us by weaving around our legs. Then, no cat. The caretaker said defensively that he had taken it to the R.S.P.C.A. to be killed. One night, the hours of waiting for the door to be opened had proved too long, and it had made a mess on a landing. The caretaker was not going to put up with *that*, he said. Bad enough clearing up after us lot, he wasn't going to clean up after cats as well.

CHAPTER FOUR

I came to live in a house in cat country. The houses are old and they have narrow gardens with walls. Through our back windows show a dozen walls one way, a dozen walls the other, of all sizes and levels. Trees, grass, bushes. There is a little theatre that has roofs at various heights. Cats thrive here. There are always cats on the walls, roofs, and in the gardens, living a complicated secret life, like the neighbourhood lives of children that go on according to unimagined private rules the grownups never guess at.

I knew there would be a cat in the house. Just as one knows, if a house is too large people will come and live in it, so certain houses must have cats. But for a while I repelled the various cats that came sniffing around to see what sort of a place it was.

During the whole of that dreadful winter of 1962, the garden and the roof over the back verandah were visited by an old black-and-white tom. He sat in the slushy snow on the roof; he prowled over the frozen ground; when the back door was briefly opened, he sat just outside, looking into the warmth. He was most unbeautiful, with a white patch over one eye, a torn ear, and a jaw always a little open and drooling. But he was not a stray. He had a good home in the street, and why he didn't stay there, no one seemed able to say.

That winter was further education into the extraordinary voluntary endurances of the English.

These houses are mostly L.C.C. owned, and by the first week of the cold, the pipes had burst and frozen, and people were waterless. The system stayed frozen.

The authorities opened a main on the street corner, and for weeks the women of the street made journeys to fetch water in jugs and cans along pavements heaped with feet of icy slush, in their house slippers. The slippers were for warmth. The slush and ice were not cleared off the pavement. They drew water from the tap, which broke down several times, and said there had been no hot water but what they boiled on the stove for one week, two weeks – then three, four and five weeks. There was, of course, no hot water for baths. When asked why they didn't complain, since after all they paid rent, they paid for water hot and cold, they replied the L.C.C. knew about their pipes, but did not do anything. The L.C.C. had pointed out there was a cold spell: they agreed with this diagnosis. Their voices were lugubrious, but they were deeply fulfilled, as this nation is when suffering entirely avoidable acts of God.

In the shop at the corner an old man, a middle-aged woman and a small child spent the days of that winter. The shop was chilled colder even than the below-zero weather nature was ordaining, by the refrigeration units; the door was always open into the iced snowdrifts outside the shop. There was no heating at all. The old man got pleurisy and went to hospital for two months. Permanently weakened, he had to sell the shop that spring. The child sat on the cement floor and cried steadily from the cold, and was slapped by its mother who stood behind the counter in a light wool dress, man's socks and a thin cardigan, saying how awful it all was, while her eyes and nose ran and her fingers swelled into chilblains. The old man next door who works as a market porter slipped on the ice outside his front door, hurt his back, and was for weeks on unemployment pay. In that house, which held nine or ten people, including two children, there was one bar of electric fire to fight the cold. Three people went to hospital, one with pneumonia.

And the pipes stayed burst, sealed in jagged stalactites of ice; the pavements remained ice slides; and the authorities did nothing. In middle-class streets, of course, snow was cleared as it fell, and the authorities responded to angry citizens demanding their rights and threatening lawsuits. In our area, people suffered it out until the spring.

Surrounded by human beings as winterbound as if they were cave dwellers of ten thousand years ago, the peculiarities of an old tomcat who chose an icy roof to spend its nights on lost their force.

In the middle of that winter, friends were offered a kitten. Friends of theirs had a Siamese cat, and she had a litter by a street cat. The hybrid kittens were being given away. Their flat is minute, and they both worked all day; but when they saw the kitten, they could not resist. During its first weekend it was fed on tinned lobster soup and chicken mousse, and it disrupted their much-married nights because it had to sleep under the chin, or at least, somewhere against the flesh, of H., the man. S., his wife, announced on the telephone that she was losing the affections of her husband to a cat, just like the wife in Colette's tale. On Monday they went off to work leaving the kitten by itself, and when they came home it was crying and sad, having been alone all day. They said they were bringing it to us. They did.

The kitten was six weeks old. It was enchanting, a delicate fairy-tale cat, whose Siamese genes showed in the shape of the face, ears, tail, and the subtle lines of its body. Her back was tabby: from above or the back, she was a pretty tabby kitten, in grey and cream. But her front and stomach were a smoky-gold, Siamese cream, with half-bars of black at the neck. Her face was pencilled with black – fine dark rings around the eyes, fine dark streaks on her cheeks, a tiny cream-coloured nose with a pink tip, outlined in black. From the front, sitting with her slender paws straight, she was an exotically beautiful beast. She sat, a tiny thing, in the middle of a yellow carpet, surrounded by five worshippers, not at all afraid of us. Then she stalked around that floor of the house, inspecting every inch of it, climbed up on to my bed, crept under the fold of a sheet, and was at home.

S. went off with H. saying: Not a moment too soon, otherwise I wouldn't have a husband at all.

And he went off groaning, saying that nothing could be as exquisite as being woken by the delicate touch of a pink tongue on his face.

The kitten went, or rather hopped, down the stairs, each of which was twice her height: first front paws, then flop, with the back; front paws, then flop with the back. She inspected the ground floor, refused the tinned food offered to her, and demanded a dirt box by mewing for it. She rejected wood shavings, but torn newspaper was acceptable, so her fastidious pose said, if there was nothing else. There wasn't: the earth outside was frozen solid.

She would not eat tinned cat food. She would not. And I was not going to feed her lobster soup and chicken. We compromised on some minced beef.

She had always been as fussy over her food as a bachelor gourmet. She gets worse as she gets older. Even as a kitten she could express annoyance, or pleasure, or a determination to sulk, by what she ate, half-ate, or chose to refuse. Her food habits are an eloquent language.

But I think it is just possible she was taken away from her mother too young. If I might respectfully suggest it to the cat experts, it is possible they are wrong when they say a kitten may leave its mother the day it turns six weeks old. This cat was six weeks, not a day more, when it was taken from its mother. The basis of her dandyism over food is the neurotic hostility and suspicion towards it of a child with food problems. She had to eat, she supposed; she did eat; but she has never eaten with enjoyment, for the sake of eating. And she shares another characteristic with people who have not had enough mother-warmth. Even now she will instinctively creep under the fold of a newspaper, or into a box or a basket – anything that shelters, anything that covers. More; she is overready to see insult; overready to sulk. And she is a frightful coward.

Kittens who are left with their mother seven or eight weeks eat easily, and they have confidence. But of course, they are not as interesting.

As a kitten, this cat never slept on the outside of the bed. She waited until I was in it, then she walked all over me, considering possibilities. She would get right down into the bed, by my feet, or on to my shoulder, or crept under the pillow. If I moved too much, she huffily changed quarters, making her annoyance felt.

When I was making the bed, she was happy to be made into it; and stayed, visible as a tiny lump, quite happily, sometimes for hours, between the blankets. If you stroked the lump, it purred and mewed. But she would not come out until she had to.

The lump would move across the bed, hesitate at the edge. There might be a frantic mew as she slid to the floor. Dignity disturbed, she licked herself hastily, glaring yellow eyes at the viewers, who made a mistake if they laughed. Then, every hair conscious of itself, she walked to some centre stage.

Time for the fastidious pernickety eating. Time for the earth box, as exquisite a performance. Time for setting the creamy fur in order. And time for play, which never took place for its own sake, but only when she was being observed.

She was as arrogantly aware of herself as a pretty girl who has no attributes but her prettiness: body and face always posed according to some inner monitor – a pose which is as good as a mask: no, no, *this* is what I am, the aggressive breasts, the sullen hostile eyes always on the watch for admiration.

Cat, at the age when, if she were human, she would be wearing clothes and hair like weapons, but confident that any time she chose she might relapse into indulged childhood again, because the role had become too much of a burden – cat posed and princessed and preened about the house and then, tired, a little peevish, tucked herself into the fold of a newspaper or behind a cushion, and watched the world safely from there.

Her prettiest trick, used mostly for company, was to lie on her back under a sofa and pull herself along by her paws, in fast sharp rushes, stopping to turn her elegant little head sideways, yellow eyes narrowed, waiting for applause. 'Oh beautiful kitten! Delicious beast! Pretty cat!' Then on she went for another display.

Or, on the right surface, the yellow carpet, a blue cushion, she lay on her back and slowly rolled, paws tucked up, head back, so that her creamy chest and stomach were exposed, marked faintly, as if she were a delicate subspecies of leopard, with black blotches, like the roses of leopards. 'Oh beautiful kitten, oh you are so beautiful.' And she was prepared to go on until the compliments stopped.

Or she sat in the back verandah, not on the table, which was unadorned, but on a little stand that had narcissus and hyacinth in earthenware pots. She sat posed between spikes of blue and white flowers, until she was noticed and admired. Not only by us, of course; also by the old rheumatic tom who prowled, grim reminder of a much harder life, around the garden where the earth was still frostbound. He saw a pretty half-grown cat, behind glass. She saw him. She lifted her head, this way, that way; bit off a fragment of hyacinth, dropped it; licked her fur, negligently; then with an insolent backwards glance, leaped down and came indoors and out of his sight. Or, on the way upstairs, on an arm or a shoulder, she would glance out of the window and see the poor old beast, so still that sometimes we thought he must have died and been frozen there. When the sun warmed a little at midday and he sat licking himself, we were relieved. Sometimes she sat watching him from the window, but her life was still to be tucked into the arms, beds, cushions, and corners of human beings.

Then the spring came, the back door was opened, the dirt box, thank goodness, made unnecessary, and the back garden became her territory. She was six months old, fully grown, from the point of view of nature.

She was so pretty then, so perfect; more beautiful even than that cat who, all those years ago, I swore could never have an equal. Well of course there hasn't been; for that cat's nature was all tact, delicacy, warmth and grace – so, as the fairy tales and the old wives say, she had to die young.

Our cat, the princess, was, still is, beautiful, but, there is no glossing it, she's a selfish beast.

The cats lined up on the garden walls. First, the sombre old winter cat, king of the back gardens. Then, a handsome black-and-white from next door, his son, from the look of it. A battle-scarred tabby. A grey-and-white cat who was so certain of defeat that he never came down from the wall. And a dashing tigerish young tom that she clearly admired. No use, the old king had not been defeated. When she strolled out, tail erect, apparently ignoring them all, but watching the handsome young tiger, he leaped down towards her, but the winter cat had only to stir where he lay on the wall, and the young cat jumped back to safety. This went on for weeks.

Meanwhile, H. and S. came to visit their lost pet. S. said how frightful and unfair it was that the princess could not have her choice; and H. said that was entirely as it should be: a princess must have a king, even if he was old and ugly. He has such dignity, said H.; he has such presence; and he had earned the pretty young cat because of his noble endurance of the long winter.

By then the ugly cat was called Mephistopheles. (In his own home, we heard, he was called Billy. Our cat had been called various names, but none of them stuck. Melissa and Franny; Marilyn and Sappho; Circe and Ayesha and Suzette. But in conversation, in love-talk, she miaowed and purred and throated in response to the long-drawn-out syllables of adjectives – beee*ooo*tiful, de*lic*ious puss.

On a very hot weekend, the only one, I seem to remember, in a nasty summer, she came in heat.

H. and S. came to lunch on the Sunday, and we sat on the back verandah and watched the choices of nature. Not ours. And not our cat's, either.

For two nights the fighting had gone on, awful fights, cats wailing and howling and screaming in the garden. Meanwhile grey puss had sat on the bottom of my bed, watching into the dark, ears lifting and moving, tail commenting, just slightly at the tip.

On that Sunday, there was only Mephistopheles in sight. Grey cat was rolling in ecstasy all over the garden. She came to us and rolled around our feet and bit them. She rushed up and down the tree at the bottom of the garden. She rolled and cried, and called, and invited.

'The most disgraceful exhibition of lust I've ever seen,' said S. watching H., who was in love with our cat.

'Oh poor cat,' said H.; 'If I were Mephistopheles I'd never treat you so badly.'

'Oh, H.,' said S., 'you are disgusting, if I told people

they'd never believe it. But I've always said, you're disgusting.'

'So that's what you've always said,' said H., caressing the ecstatic cat.

It was a very hot day, we had a lot of wine for lunch, and the love play went on all afternoon.

Finally, Mephistopheles leaped down off the wall to where grey cat was wriggling and rolling – but alas, he bungled it.

'Oh my God,' said H., genuinely suffering. 'It is really not forgivable, that sort of thing.'

S., anguished, watched the torments of our cat, and doubted, frequently, dramatically and loudly, whether sex was worth it. 'Look at it,' said she, 'that's us. That's what we're like.'

'That's not at all what we're like,' said H. 'It's Mephistopheles. He should be shot.'

Shoot him at once, we all said; or at least lock him up so that the young tiger from next door could have his chance.

But the handsome young cat was not visible.

We went on drinking wine; the sun went on shining; our princess danced, rolled, rushed up and down the tree, and, when at last things went well, was clipped again and again by the old king.

'All that's wrong,' said H., 'is that he's too old for her.'

'Oh my God,' said S., 'I'm going to take you home. Because if I don't, I swear you'll make love to that cat yourself.'

'Oh I wish I could,' said H. 'What an exquisite beast, what a lovely creature, what a princess, she's wasted on a cat, I can't stand it.'

Next day winter returned; the garden was cold and wet; and grey cat had returned to her fastidious disdainful ways. And the old king lay on the garden wall in the slow English rain, still victor of them all, waiting.

CHAPTER FIVE

Grey puss wore her pregnancy lightly. She raced down the garden and up the tree and back; then again, and again; the point of this being the moment when, clamped to the tree, she turned her head, eyes half-closed, to receive applause. She jumped down the stairs three, four at a time. She pulled herself along the floor under the sofa. And, since she had learned that any person, at first sight of her, was likely to go into ecstasies: Oh what a beautiful cat! – she was always near the front door when guests arrived, suitably posed.

Then, trying to slide through banisters to drop on to a stair the flight below, she found she could not. She tried again, could not. She was humiliated, pretended she had not tried, that she preferred walking the long way around the bends in the stairway.

Her rushes up and down the tree became slower, then stopped.

And when the kittens moved in her belly, she looked surprised, put out.

Usually, about a fortnight before the birth, a cat will go sniffing into cupboards and corners: trying out, rejecting, choosing. This cat did nothing of the kind. I cleared shoes out of a cupboard in the bedroom, and showed her the place – sheltered, dark, comfortable. She walked into it and out again. Other places were offered. It was not that she did not like them; it seemed that she didn't know what was happening.

The day before the birth, she did roll herself around some old newspapers in a seat, but the actions she used were automatic, nothing purposeful about them. Some gland, or whatever it is, had spoken, prompted movements; she obeyed, but what she did was not connected with her vital knowledge, or so it seemed, for she did not try again.

On the day of the birth she was in labour for three hours or so before she knew it. She miaowed, sounding surprised, sitting on the kitchen floor, and when I ordered her upstairs to the cupboard she went. She did not stay there. She trotted vaguely around the house, sniffing, at this late stage, into various possible places, but lost interest, and came down to the kitchen again. The pain, or sensation, having lessened, she forgot it, and was prepared to start ordinary life again – the life of a pampered, adored kitten. After all, she still was one.

I took her up, and made her stay in the cupboard. She did not want to. She simply did not have any of the expected reactions. In fact, she was touching, absurd – and funny, and we wanted to laugh. When the contractions grew strong, she was cross. When she had a bad pain towards the end, she miaowed, but it was a protesting, annoyed miaow. She was annoyed with us, who concurred in this process being inflicted on her.

It is fascinating to watch the birth of a cat's first kitten, that moment, when, the tiny writhing creature having appeared in its envelope of white cellophane, the cat licks off the covering, nips at the cord, eats the afterbirth, all so cleanly, so efficiently, so perfectly, actions performed by her, personally, for the first time. Always there is a moment of pause. The kitten is expelled, lies at the cat's back end. The cat looks, with a trapped, wanting-to-escape reflex, at the new thing attached to her; she looks again, she does not know what it is; then the mechanism works, and she obeys, becomes mother, purrs, is happy.

With this cat there was the longest pause I've seen while she looked at the new kitten. She looked, looked at me, moved a little, to see if she could lose the attached object – then it worked. She cleaned the kitten, did everything expected of her, purred – and then she got up and walked downstairs, where she sat on the back verandah looking at the garden. *That* was over, she seemed to be thinking. Then her sides contracted again, and she turned around to look at me – she was annoyed, furious. Her face, the lines of her body said, unmistakably, What a damned nuisance! Go upstairs! I ordered. Upstairs! She went, sulking. She crept up those stairs with her ears back – *almost* as a dog does when it is being scolded or in disgrace: but she had none of the abjectness of a dog. On the contrary, she was irritated with me and with the whole process. When she saw the first kitten again, she recognized it, again the machinery worked, and she licked it. She gave birth to four kittens in all, and went to sleep, a charming picture, exquisite cat curled around four feeding kittens. They were a fine lot. The first, female, a replica of her, even to the pencilled dark rings around the eyes, the black half-bands on the chest and legs, the creamy, faintly marked stomach. Then a greyish-blue kitten: later, in certain lights, it looked dark purple. A black kitten, when grown a perfect black cat, with yellow eyes, all elegance and strength. And the father's kitten, exactly like him, a rather heavy graceless kitten, in black and white. The first three had the light lines of the Siamese strain.

When the cat woke up, she looked at the kittens, now asleep, got up, shook herself, and strolled downstairs. She drank some milk, ate some raw meat, licked herself all over. She did not go back to the litter.

S. and H., coming to admire the kittens, found mamma cat, posed on the bottom of the stairs in profile. Then she ran out of the house, up the tree and back again – several times. Then she went up to the top of the house, and came all the way down by dropping through the banisters of one flight, to the flight below. Then she wove around H.'s legs, purring.

'You are supposed to be a mother,' said S., shocked. 'Why aren't you with your kittens?'

It seemed she had forgotten the kittens. Inexplicably, she had had an uncomfortable job to do; she had done it; it was over, and that was that. She frisked and fro-licked around the house until, late that night, I ordered her upstairs. She would not go. I picked her up and carried her to the kittens. With no grace at all, she got in with them. She would not lie down to feed them. I made her. As soon as I turned away, she left them. I sat with her as she fed them.

I went to get ready for bed. When I came back to the bedroom, she was under my sheet, asleep. I returned her to the kittens. She looked at them with her ears back, and again would have simply walked off, if I had not stood over her, pointing, inexorable figure of author-ity, at the kittens. She went in, slumped down, as if to say, if you insist. Once the kittens were at her nipples instinct did work, even if ineffectually, and she purred for a while.

All through the night she was sneaking out of the cupboard and getting into her usual place on my bed. Every time I made her go back. As soon as I was asleep, back she came, while the kittens complained.

She had understood, by morning, that she was re-sponsible for those kittens. But left to herself, that great Mother, nature, notwithstanding, she would let them starve.

Next day, when we were at lunch, grey cat ran into the room with a kitten, tossing it up and down in her mouth. She put the kitten in the middle of the floor, and went up for the others. She brought the four down, one after another, then she lay stretched out on the kitchen floor with them. She was not going to be shut away by herself away from company, she had decided; and through the month the kittens were helpless, any one of us, anywhere in the house, would see grey cat trotting into the room with her kittens tossing them about in her mouth in what seemed to be the most appallingly careless way. At night, whenever I woke, grey cat would be tucked in at my side, silent, and she stayed silent, hoping I would not notice her. When she knew I had, she purred, hoping I would soften, and licked my face and bit my nose. All no use. I ordered her back, and she went, sulking.

In short, she was a disastrous mother. We put it down to her youth. When those kittens were a day old, she was trying to play with them as a cat does with kittens a month or five weeks old. A minute, blind blob of a kitten would be buffeted about by those great hind feet; and bitten in tender play, while all it wanted was to get to the grudgingly offered nipples. A sad sight, granted; and we all got cross with her; and then we laughed, but that was worse, because if there is one thing she won't have, it is being laughed at.

In spite of their bad treatment, that first litter were enchanting, the best produced in this house, each remarkable of its kind, even the replica of old Mephistopheles.

One day I came upstairs and found him in the bedroom. He was looking at the kittens. Grey cat, of course, was not there. He was some feet off, his head poked foward, his drooling jaw open as usual. But he did not want to harm them, he was interested.

The kittens, being so attractive, at once found homes. But they were a sad litter, after all. Inside eighteen months, they all came to grief. The much-loved cat who was its mother's image disappeared from its home one day and was never found. And so with the black cat. Baby Mephistopheles was taken off, for his strength and courage, to be a cat in a warehouse, but died of cat enteritis. Purple cat, having given birth to the most remarkable litter I've seen, three perfect Siamese kittens, cream-coloured, pink-eyed, and three London scruff, little ragbags, lost her home. But we hear she has found another in a nearby street.

Grey cat, we decided, should not be allowed to have kittens again. She simply was not suited for motherhood. But it was too late. She was pregnant again. Not by Mephistopheles.

This area is known as cat country to the cat dealers and stealers. I suppose they drive around it and take any animals they like the look of which are not safely indoors. It happens at night; and it is unpleasant to think how the thieves keep the cats quiet so that they don't wake their owners. The people of this street suspect the hospitals by which we are surrounded. Those vivisectionists have been again, they say; and perhaps they are right. Anyway one night six cats disappeared, among them Mephistopheles. And now the grey cat had her fancy, the tigerish young tom with a white satin vest.

Again the birth took her by surprise, but it did not take so long for her to settle down. She got up from the accouchement and went downstairs and would not have gone back unless ordered; but on the whole I think she enjoyed that second litter. This time the kittens were ordinary, pretty enough mixtures of tabby and white-and-tabby, but they had no special qualities of line or colour, and it was harder to find them homes.

Autumn, the paths thick with brown sycamore leaves from the big tree: cat taught her four kittens to hunt and stalk and jump while the leaves drifted down. The leaves played the part of mice and birds – and then were brought into the house. One of the kittens would very carefully shred his leaf to bits. This is how he inherited grey cat's oddest trait: she will spend half an hour methodically ripping up a newspaper with her teeth, piece after piece. Perhaps this is a Siamese characteristic? I have a friend with two Siamese cats. When she has roses in the flat, the cats will take roses out of the vase with their teeth, lay them down, and tear the petals off, one by one, as if engaged in a necessary job of work. Perhaps in nature, the leaf, the newspaper, the rose would have been materials for a lair.

Grey cat enjoyed teaching her kittens the arts of hunting. If they had been country cats, they would have been well educated. Also, she taught them cleanliness: none of her kittens ever dirtied a corner. But, still a fussy eater, she was not interested in teaching them to eat. That they learned for themselves.

Of this litter, one was left much longer than the others. For the winter we had two cats, grey cat and her son, who was a rich-coloured browny-orange cat, with a vest like his father.

Grey cat became a kitten again, and these two played together all day, and slept wrapped around each other. The young tom was much bigger than its mother; but she bullied him, and beat him when he displeased her. They would lie for hours licking each other's faces and purring.

He was an enormous eater, ate everything. We hoped his example would teach her better sense with her food, but it did not. She would always, as cats do, let him, her child, eat and drink first, while she crouched watching. When he was finished, she went over, sniffed at the cat food or the scraps, and then came to me, and very delicately bit my calf to remind me that she ate rabbit, raw meat, or raw fish, in small portions properly served on a clean saucer.

Over this – her due, her right – she would crouch aggressively, glaring at him, eating just so much and no more, without haste. She seldom finishes all the food put down for her; nearly aways leaves a bit – suburban good manners, which, observed thus, in a different context, with grey cat, occurs to me for the first time must have a basis in really nasty aggression. 'I'm not going to finish this food – I'm not hungry, and you've cooked too much and it's your fault it's wasted.' 'I have so much to eat, I don't need to eat this.' 'I'm a delicate superior creature and really above crude things like food.' The last is grey cat's statement.

The young tom ate what she left, not noticing that it was much nicer than what he had been given; and then they rushed off, chasing each other through the house and garden. Or they sat on the bottom of my bed, looking out of the window, licking each other from time to time, and purring.

This was grey cat's apogee, the peak of her happiness and charm. She was not lonely; her companion did not threaten her, because she dominated him. And she was so beautiful – really so very beautiful.

She was best sitting on the bed looking out. Her two creamy lightly barred front legs were straight down side by side, on two silvery paws. Her ears, lightly fringed with white that looked silver, lifted and moved, back, forward, listening and sensing. Her face turned, slightly, after each new sensation, alert. Her tail moved, in another dimension, as if its tip was catching messages her other organs could not. She sat poised, air-light, looking, hearing, feeling, smelling, breathing, with all of her, fur, whiskers, ears – everything, in delicate vibration. If a fish is the movement of water embodied, given shape, then cat is a diagram and pattern of subtle air.

Oh cat; I'd say, or pray: be-*oooo*tiful cat! Delicious cat! Exquisite cat! Satiny cat! Cat like a soft owl, cat with paws like moths, jewelled cat, miraculous cat! Cat, cat, cat, cat.

She would ignore me first; then turn her head, silkily

arrogant, and half close her eyes for each praise-name, each one separately. And, when I'd finished, yawn, deliberate, foppish, showing an ice-cream-pink mouth and curled pink tongue.

Or, deliberate, she would crouch and fascinate me with her eyes. I stared into them, almond-shaped in their fine outline of dark pencil, around which was a second pencilling of cream. Under each, a brush stroke of dark. Green, green eyes; but in shadow, a dark smoky gold – a dark-eyed cat. But in the light, green, a clear cool emerald. Behind the transparent globes of the eyeball, slices of veined gleaming butterfly wing. Wings like jewels – the essence of wing.

A leaf insect is not to be distinguished from a leaf – at a casual glance. But then, look close: the copy of a leaf is more leaf than leaf – furled, veined, delicate, as if a jeweller had worked it, but a jeweller with his tongue very slightly in his cheek, so that the insect is on the verge of mockery. Look, says the leaf insect, the fake: has any leaf ever been as exquisite as I am? Why, even where I have copied the imperfections of a leaf, I am perfect. Do you ever want to look at a mere leaf again, having seen me, the artifice?

In grey cat's eyes lay the green sheen of a jade butterfly's wing, as if an artist had said: what could be as graceful, as delicate as a cat? What more naturally the creature of the air? What air-being has affinity with cat? Butterfly, butterfly of course! And there, deep in cat's eyes lies this thought, hinted at merely, with a half-laugh; and hidden behind the fringes of lashes, behind the fine brown inner lid, and the evasions of cat-coquetry.

Grey cat, perfect, exquisite, a queen; grey cat with her hints of leopard and snake; suggestions of butterfly and owl; a miniature lion steel-clawed for murder, grey cat full of secrets, affinities, mysteries – grey cat, eighteen months old, a young matron in her prime, had a third litter of kittens, this time by the grey-and-white cat who, during the reign of the king, had been too frightened to come down off the wall. She had four kittens, and her son sat beside her through the birth and watched, licking her in the pauses of labour, and licking the kittens. He tried to get into the nest with them, but his ears were boxed for this lapse into infantilism.

CHAPTER SIX

It was spring again, the back door was open, and grey cat, her grown son and four kittens enjoyed the garden. But grey cat preferred the company of her son to the kittens; and indeed, had again scandalized S. because, the moment her labour was over, she got up, walked off from the kittens, and then fell straight into her grown son's arms, when they rolled over and over, purring.

He played the role of father to this litter: he brought them up as much as she did.

Meanwhile there had already appeared, faint and disguised, as the future always is in its first intimations, the shadow of grey cat's doom as reigning and sole queen of the household.

Above, in the human world, frightful storms and emotions and dramas; and with the summer a beautiful sad blonde girl visited the house, and she had a small neat elegant black cat, a half-kitten really, and this alien was in the basement, only temporarily of course, because her own home was not available.

The little black cat had a red collar and a red leash, and at this stage of her life was only an appurtenance and a decorative asset to the beautiful girl. She was kept well away from the queen upstairs: they were not allowed to meet.

Then, all at once, things went wrong for grey cat. Her son was at last claimed by the person who had booked him, and went off to live in Kensington. The four kittens went to their new homes. And we decided it was enough, she should have no more kittens.

I did not then know what neutering a female cat

involved. People I knew had 'doctored' cats, male and female. The R.S.P.C.A., when asked, emphatically advised it. Understandably: they have to destroy hundreds of unwanted cats every week – every one of which, I suppose, has been to someone 'Oh what a lovely kitten' – until it grew up. But in the voices of the ladies of the R.S.P.C.A. sounded exactly the same note as in the voice of the woman at the corner grocery who, when I went around looking for homes for kittens, always said: 'Haven't you had her done *yet*? Poor thing, making her go through that, I think it's cruel.' 'But it's natural to have kittens,' I insisted, dishonestly enough, since any instincts of maternity grey cat had were bullied into her.

My relations with the ladies of the street have mostly been about cats – cats lost or visiting, or kittens to be visited by children, or kittens about to be theirs. And there is not one who hasn't insisted that it is cruel to let a cat have kittens – with vehemence, with hysteria, or at the very least with the sullen last-ditch antagonism of my mother's: 'It's all very well for you!'

The old bachelor who ran the vegetable shop at the corner – now closed because of the pressure of the supermarket, and because he said his was a family business and he had no family – a fat old boy with cheeks red-purple, almost black, like the old woman of the fruit and vegetable barrows, said about the women: 'They never stop having kids, but they don't look after them, do they?' He had no children, and was self-righteous about everyone else's.

He did have, however, an ancient mother, over eighty, completely bedridden, who must have everything done for her – by him. His brother and three sisters were married and had children and it was his job, they decided, the unmarried brother's job, to look after the old mother, since their children gave them enough to do.

He stood in his tiny shop behind racks of swedes,

turnips, potatoes, onions, carrots, cabbages – other vegetables, as happens in such streets, being unobtainable unless frozen – and watched the children rushing about the streets, saying unkind things about their mothers.

He was in favour of the grey cat's being 'done'. Too many people in the world, too many animals, too little food, nobody bought anything these days, where would it all end?

I rang up three vets to ask if it was necessary for a cat's womb and tubes to be removed – could they not tie up her tubes and leave her sex, at least? All three, with emphasis, insisted the best thing was to have the whole lot out. 'The whole job lot,' said one; exactly the same phrase was used to a woman friend of mine by a gynaecologist. 'I'll get rid of the whole job lot for you,' said he.

Very interesting.

In Portugal, say H. and S., who are Portuguese, when the bourgeois ladies visit for their tea parties, they talk about their operations and their female problems. The phrase they use for these organs is exactly the same as that used for fowl giblets: 'My giblets, your giblets, our giblets.'

Very interesting indeed.

I put the grey cat in the cat basket and took her to the vet. She had never been shut up before, and she complained – her dignity and self-respect were wounded. I left her, and came back late that afternoon to collect her.

She was in the cat basket, smelling of ether, limp, dizzy, sick. A large patch had been shaved off one side, exposing her whitish-grey skin. Across the skin a two-inch red gash, sewn up neatly with gut. She looked at me with enormous dark shocked eyes. She had been betrayed and she knew it. She had been sold out by a friend, the person who fed her, protected her, whose bed she slept on. A terrible thing had been done to her. I couldn't bear to look at her eyes. I took her home in a taxi, where she moaned all the way – a hopeless helpless frightened sound. At home, I put her in another basket, not the cat basket with its memories of the vet and pain. I covered her, put the basket by a radiator, and sat with her. It was not that she was very ill, or in danger. She was in a bad state of shock. I do not think any creature can 'get over' an experience like this.

She stayed there, not moving at all, for two days. Then, with difficulty, she used the cat box. She drank a little milk and crept back to lie down.

At the end of a week the stubble grew back over the ugly scarred patch. Soon I had to take her back to the vet to have her stitches taken out. This was worse than the first journey, because now she knew the basket, the motions of the car, meant pain and terror.

She screamed and struggled in the basket. The taxi man, as helpful as they always are, in my experience, stopped his taxi for a while to let me try and soothe her, but then we agreed it was better to get it over with. I waited while the stitches came out. She was forced, struggling, back into the basket, and I brought her back in the same taxi. She made water from fear, and cried. The taxi-man, a cat-lover, said why couldn't those doctors invent a birth control for cats? It was not right, he said, for us to steal their real natures from them, to suit our convenience.

When I got inside the door and opened the basket, grey cat, mobile now, fled out of the house and on to the garden wall under the tree, her eyes again wide and shocked. She came in at night to eat. And slept, not on my bed, but on the sofa. She would not let herself be petted for days.

Inside a month from the date of that operation, her shape changed. She lost, not slowly, but fast, her slenderness, her grace; and she coarsened everywhere. Her eyes subtly loosened, crinkled; the shape of her face broadened. She was, all at once, a plump, if pretty, cat.

As for the change in her nature, well, that might have been, probably was, partly due to the other blows life dealt her at the same time – losing her friend, the young tom, losing her kittens, and the advent of the black cat.

But it did change. Her confidence had been struck. The tyrannical beauty of the household had vanished. The peremptory charm, the heart-breaking tricks of head and eye – all gone. She did, of course, return to old cajoleries, rolling back and forth on her back to be admired, pulling herself under the sofa – but they were tentative for a long time. She was not *sure* they would please. She was not sure of anything for a long time. And so, she insisted. A strident note entered her character. She was tetchy over her rights. She was spiteful. She had to be humoured. She was bad-tempered with her old admirers, the toms on the walls. In short, she had turned into a spinster cat. It is a dreadful thing we do to these beasts. But I suppose we have to do it.

CHAPTER SEVEN

The little black cat, for a variety of sad reasons, was homeless and joined our household. It would have been better for harmony if she had been a male cat. As it was, the two she-cats met as enemies, crouched watching each other for hours.

Grey cat, half her side still stubbly from the razor, refusing to sleep on my bed, refusing to eat until coaxed, unhappy and unsure of herself, was determined about one thing: that the black cat was not going to take her place.

Black cat, on her side, knew she was going to live here, and would not be chased away. She did not fight: grey cat was bigger and stronger. She got into the corner of a seat, her back protected by a wall, and never took her eyes off grey cat.

When her enemy went to sleep, black cat ate and drank. Then she surveyed the garden with which she had already become acquainted from the end of a smart leash and collar, examined it carefully. Then she examined the house, floor by floor. My bed, she decided, was the place for her. At which grey cat leaped up, spitting, and chased the black cat away, took her place on my bed. Black cat then took up a position on the sofa.

Black cat's character is altogether different from grey cat's. She is a steady, obstinate, modest little beast. She knew no coquetry until she saw grey cat's: did not pose, flirt, roll, scamper, or show off.

She knew she was not the first cat of the household; grey cat was the boss cat. But as second cat she had rights, and insisted on them. The two cats never fought, physically. They fought great duels with their eyes. On either side of the kitchen they sat; green eyes, yellow eyes staring. If black cat did something over the edge of what grey cat thought was tolerable, grey cat gave a faint growl, and made subtle threatening movements with her muscles. Black cat desisted. Grey cat slept on my bed; black cat must not. Grey cat could sit on the table; but not black cat. When visitors came, grey cat was first at the door. And grey cat would not eat, unless separately, out of a newly washed saucer, with newly cut food, and in a fresh place in the kitchen. For black cat, the old food corner would do.

Black cat submitted to all this, and with the humans in the house was modestly affectionate, wreathed our legs, purred, talked – she is half-Siamese too; but always with an eye on grey cat.

This behaviour did not accord with her appearance. Grey cat's looks and her behaviour have always gone together: her looks have dictated her character.

But black cat is ambiguous. For instance, her size. She is a small slender cat. When she has kittens, it seems incredible there could be room for them. But pick her up: she is solid, heavy; a strong close-packed little beast. She does not look at all modest, domestic; and as maternal as she later turned out to be.

She is elegant. She has a curved noble profile, like a cat on a tomb. When she sits straight, paws side by side, staring, or crouches, eyes half-masked, she is still, remote, withdrawn to some distant place inside herself. At such times she is sombre, inspires awe. And she is black, black, black. Black glossy whiskers, black lashes, not a white hair anywhere. If grey cat's designer was a master of subtlety, of loving detail, then black cat's said: I shall create a black cat, the quintessence of black cat, a cat from the Underworld.

It took about two weeks for these antagonists to

establish rules of precedence. They never touched, or played, or licked each other: they created a balance where they were always conscious of each other, in watchful hostility. And that was sad, remembering how grey cat and her grown child had played and cleaned each other and wound about each other. Perhaps, we thought, these two might learn affection in time.

But then black cat got sick, and poor grey cat's hard-fought-for position was lost completely.

Black cat had a cold, I thought. Her bowels were out of order: she made frequent trips to the garden. She was sick several times.

If I had taken her to the doctor then, she would not have been so very ill. She had enteritis; but I did not know how bad that is, and that very few cats get over it, not, at least, while they are still half-kitten. On the second night of her illness I woke and saw her crouched in a corner – coughing, I thought at first. But she was trying to be sick – with nothing left to be sick with. Her jaws and mouth were covered with white froth, a sticky foam which would not easily wipe off. I washed it off. She went back to the corner, crouching, looking in front of her. The way she sat was ominous: immobile, patient, and she was not asleep. She was waiting.

In the morning I took her to the cat hospital around the corner, by now bitten by remorse because I had not taken her earlier. She was very ill, they said; and from the way they said it, I knew she was not expected to live. She was badly dehydrated and had a roaring tempera-ture. They gave her an injection for the fever, and said she must be made to take liquid – if possible. She would not drink, I said. No, they would not, they said, past a certain stage in the illness, which was characterized by another symptom: cats decide to die. They creep into a cool place somewhere, because of the heat of their blood, crouch down, and wait to die.

When I took black cat home, she stalked gauntly into the garden. It was early autumn and cold. She crouched against the chill of the garden wall, cold earth under her, in the patient waiting position of the night before.

I carried her in, and put her on a blanket, not too close to a radiator. She went back to the garden: same position, same deadly, patient position.

I took her back and shut her in. She crept to the door, and settled down there, nose towards it, waiting to die.

I tempted her with water, water and glucose, meat juices. It wasn't that she refused them: she had gone beyond them; food was something that she had left behind. She did not want to come back; she would not.

Next day the people at the hospital said her temperature was still very high. It had not come down. And she *must* drink.

I brought her home and thought it out. Clearly, keeping black cat alive would be a full-time job. And I was busy. And, as people in the house were pointing out, she was only a cat.

But she was *not* just a cat. For a variety of reasons, all of them human and irrelevant to her, she must not be allowed to die.

I mixed a nasty but useful solution of glucose, blood and water, and fought black cat.

She would not open her jaws to take it. A small feverish creature, shadow-light, having lost all her healthy solidity of flesh, she sat, or rather, collapsed, in my lap, and shut her teeth against the spoon. It was the strength of weakness: no, no, no.

I forced her teeth open, using her canines as levers. The liquid was in her throat, but she would not swallow. I held her jaws up, and the liquid ran out of the sides of her mouth. But some of it must have gone down, because after the third, fourth, fifth spoonful, she made a faint swallowing movement.

57

So that was it. Every half hour. I took the poor creature from her corner, and forced liquid down her. I was afraid of hurting her jaw, because of using so much pressure on her projecting teeth. Her jaw was probably very painful.

That night I put her by me on the bed, and woke her every hour. Though she was not really asleep. She crouched, the heat from the fever sending waves all around her, eyes half-open, suffering the end of her life.

Next day the fever had still not gone down. But the day after it had; and now the clinic gave her glucose injections. Each injection left a large soft bulge under her stiff hide. But she did not care; she cared about nothing at all.

Now that the fever was gone, she was very cold. I wrapped her in an old towel, and put her near the radiator. Every half hour, black cat and I fought. Or rather, black cat's intention to die fought with my intention that she should not.

At night, she crouched by me on the bed, trembling with the sad faint inner trembling of extreme weakness, a towel over her. Wherever I put her she stayed; she did not have the strength to move. But she would *not* open her jaws to take liquid. She would not. All her remaining strength went into saying *no*.

Ten days went by. I took her to the cat hospital every day. It was a place where young vets are trained, a teaching hospital. The people of the neighbourhood take dogs and cats every morning, between nine and twelve. We sat on rows of benches in a large bare waiting-room, with the sick animals fretting, whining, barking. All kinds of friendships were struck up on account of the illnesses of these animals.

And all kinds of small sad incidents stay in my mind. For instance, there was a woman, middle-aged, her hair dyed light blonde, over a haggard face. She had the most beautiful large dog which was sleek with food and attention. There could not have been much wrong with the dog, which was lively, and barked and was proud of itself. But the woman stood in a light suit, always the same suit, without a coat. It was a little cold, not very, and the rest of us wore light dresses or sweaters. But she shivered uncontrollably; the flesh on her arms and legs was not there. It was clear that she did not have enough to eat, and that her money and time went on the dog. To feed a dog of that size costs a lot of money. A cat costs, I reckon, ten shillings a week, even if it isn't a spoiled beast, as ours both are. That woman lived through her dog. I think everyone felt it. The people in this area are mostly poor: the way they looked at her, shivering there with her pampered beast, and then invited her to jump the queue to get out of the cold into the building while we waited for the doors to open, said that they understood her situation and were sorry for her.

And an incident at the other extreme – or apparently so. A fat bulldog – but very fat, rolls of flesh all over it – was brought in by a fat boy of about twelve. The doctors had the dog on the examination table, and explained to the boy that a dog must eat just so much, and only once a day: there was nothing wrong with it but overfeeding. And it must not be fed bits of cake and bread and sweets and . . . The fat boy repeated, over and over again, that he would go back and tell his mother, he would tell his mother, he said; but what *she* wanted to know was, why did the dog wheeze and pant, after all, it was only two years old, and it would not run and play and bark as other dogs did. Well, said the doctors patiently, it was as easy to overfeed an animal as to underfeed it. If you overfed a dog, you see . . .

Extraordinarily patient they are; and very kind. And tactful. The things that must be done to animals which

59

would upset their owners take place behind closed doors. Poor black cat was taken off for her injections and was gone twenty minutes, half an hour, before being returned to me with the subcutaneous water lumping her stiff dirty fur.

She had not licked herself, cleaned herself, for days. She could not move. She was not getting better. If all my attention, if all the skills of the clinic made no difference, well, perhaps after all she should be allowed to die, since that was what she wanted. There she sat, day after day, under the radiator. Her fur was already like a dead cat's, with dust and fluff in it; her eyes were gummy; the fur around her mouth was solid with the glucose I tried to pour into her.

I thought of what it was like being sick in bed, the feeling of irritable disgust, of self-hatred that sets in, until it seems to be the illness itself. One's hair needs washing; one can smell the sourness of illness on one's breath, one's skin. One seems shut inside a shell of sickness, a miasma of illness. Then along comes the nurse, washes one's face, brushes one's hair, and whisks away sour-smelling sheets.

No, of course cats are not human; humans are not cats; but all the same, I couldn't believe that such a fastidious little beast as black cat was not suffering from the knowledge of how dirty and smelly she was.

But you can't wash a cat. First I took a light towel wrung out in hot water, and rubbed her with it, gently, all over, to get rid of the dirt and fluff and stickiness. This took a long time. She remained passive, suffered probably, because by now her skin was punctured by so many injections. Then, when she was warm, fur and ears and eyes, I dried her with a warmed towel.

And then – and I think it was this that made the difference – I made my hands warm by heating them in hot water, and I rubbed her, very slowly, all over. I tried to rub some life into her cold body. I did this for some time, about half an hour.

When it was finished, I covered her with a clean warm towel. And then, very stiff and slow, she got up and walked across the kitchen. She soon crouched down again, where the impulse to move had ebbed out. But she *had* moved, of her own accord.

Next day I asked the doctors if rubbing the cat might have made some difference. They said, probably not, they thought it was the injections. However that may be, there is no doubt the point where there was a possibility of her living came when she was cleaned and rubbed. For another ten days she was given glucose by the clinic; forced to take the nasty mixtures of meat juices, water and glucose by me; and rubbed and brushed twice a day.

And all this time, poor grey cat was pushed on one side. First things first. Black cat needed too much attention for grey cat to be given much. But grey cat was not going to accept handouts, no second-best for her. She simply removed herself, physically and emotionally, and watched. Sometimes she came cautiously to black cat, to all intents and purposes already dead, sniffed at her, and backed away. Sometimes her hair lifted as she sniffed at black cat. Once or twice, during the time black cat was creeping out into the cold garden to die, grey cat went too, and sat a few paces away watching her. But she did not seem to be hostile; she did not try to hurt black cat.

During all that time, grey cat never played, or did her tricks, or made special demands over her food. She was not petted, and she slept in the corner of the bedroom on the floor, not rolled up into a luxurious ball, but crouching to watch the bed where black cat was being nursed.

Then black cat began to recover, and the worst period started – that is, from the human point of view. And perhaps for black cat too, who had been bullied back into life against her will. She was like a kitten who had to do everything new, or like a very old person. She had no control of her bowels: had forgotten, it seemed, the function of dirt boxes. She ate painfully, clumsily, and made messes as she ate. And wherever she was, she might suddenly collapse, and sit crouching and staring in front of her. Very upsetting it was: the small sick aloof beast, always sitting in a stiff crouch, never rolled up, or stretched out. And staring – a deathlike cat she looked, with her staring distant eyes. For a while I thought she might have gone a little crazy.

But she got better. She stopped messing floors. She ate. And one day, instead of settling into her usual waiting crouch, she remembered that one could lie curled. It did not come easily or at once. She made two or three attempts, as if her muscles could not remember how the thing was done. Then, she curled herself up, nose to tail, and slept. She was a cat again.

But she still had not licked herself. I tried to remind her by taking a forepaw and rubbing it over her cheek, but she let it drop. It was too soon.

I had to go away for a six-week trip, and the cats were left with a friend to look after them.

When I came back into the kitchen, grey cat was sitting on the table, boss cat again. And on the floor was black cat, glossy, sleek, clean and purring.

The balance of power had been restored. And black cat had forgotten she had been ill. But not quite. Her muscles have never quite recovered. There is a stiffness in her haunches: she can't jump cleanly, though well enough. On her back above her tail is a thin patch of fur. And somewhere in her brain is held a memory of that time. Over a year later I took her to the clinic because she had a minor ear infection. She did not mind being carried there in the basket. She did not mind the waiting-room. But when she was carried into the diagnosing room, she began to tremble and to salivate. They took her into the inside room, where she had had so many injections, to clean her ears, and when she was brought back, she was rigid with fright, her mouth streaming, and she trembled for hours afterwards. But she is a normal cat, with normal instincts.

CHAPTER EIGHT

Perhaps it is because she was so near death, but black cat's appetites are enormous: in black cat we are witnessing the redressing of a balance.

She eats three or four times as much as grey cat, and when she is on heat, she is formidable. Grey cat was luxuriously amorous. Black cat is obsessed. For four or five days, the humans watch, awed, this singleminded force of nature. Black cat announces the onset of her need for a mate in a frenzied purring, rolling and demand to be petted. She makes love to our feet, to the carpet, to a hand. Black cat yowls around the garden. Black cat complains at the top of her voice that it is not enough, *not* enough – and then, sex no longer being her concern, she is a mother, full time and a hundred per cent, with never an impulse towards anything else.

The father of black cat's first litter was a new cat, a young tabby. That summer there was a new population of cats. The vivisectionists, or the cat-fur suppliers, had made another haul in our block, and six cats had disappeared overnight.

There were available: the handsome tabby; a long-haired black-and-white cat; a white cat with grey patches. She wanted the tabby, and she got the tabby. With supplements. Towards the end of the second day of her being on heat, I observed the following scene.

Black cat had been under the tabby for some hours. She came running in to the hall, wanting to be chased. There she rolled over, waiting. The tabby came in after her, looked at her, licked her, then as she rolled and coaxed, pinned her down with a paw, as if to say, be quiet for a minute. Indulgent, affectionate, there he crouched, pinning down the importunate black cat. Under his paw she wriggled and pleaded. Be quiet, said he. Then she wriggled free, and chased out into the garden, looking back to see if he followed. He did follow, taking his time. In the garden waited the black-and-white cat. Our cat rolled and enticed the tabby, who sat, apparently indifferent, licking his fur. But he was watching her. She began to roll in front of the black-and-white cat. The tabby cat went over and crouched by the pair, watching. He sat there, observing, while black cat mated with black-and-white cat. It was a short mating. When black cat got free of her new mate, purely for the purpose of coquetry, tabby cat punished her for infidelity by boxing her ears. He got on top of her himself. At no point did he take any notice of, or punish, the black-and-white cat, who from time to time during those three, four days took a turn with black cat, whose ears got boxed, but without much emphasis.

Cats have a double uterus, like rabbits. Black cat had six kittens. There was one greyish kitten, two black ones, three black-and-white, so it looked as if the second-string mate had more effect on the kittens than the favoured tabby.

Like grey cat, black cat is very far from the natural law which says kittens should be born in a dark hidden place. She likes to have kittens in a room which is always inhabited. At that time, the room at the top of the house was used by a girl who was studying for examinations, and therefore mostly in. Black cat chose her leather chair, and gave birth while grey cat watched. Once or twice grey cat climbed up on the arm of the chair, and put down a paw to touch a kitten. But in this area, the maternal, black cat is sure of herself and commands grey cat, who was made to get down.

The kittens were born properly, neatly, and with

dispatch. As usual we went through the awful business, as there appeared one, two, three, four, five, six kittens, of hoping that each one would be the last, hoping that just this once she might have two, perhaps three. As usual we decided that three would be enough, we would dispose of the rest, and then, when they were clean, standing up, front paws on mamma's chest, vigorously nursing while she purred and was proud of herself, decided that we could not possibly kill them.

Unlike grey cat, she hated to leave them; and was best pleased where there were four or five people around the chair, admiring her. When grey cat yawns, accepting homage, she is insolent, languid. Black cat, among kittens, told she is clever and beautiful, yawns happily, without self-consciousness, very pink mouth and pink tongue against the black, black fur.

Black cat, mother, is fearless. When there are kittens in the house, and other cats invade, black cat hurls herself down the stairs and rushes screeching after them: they go pelting off and over the walls.

But grey cat, if an unwelcome cat appears, will growl and threaten and warn until a human comes. Then, supported, she rushes after the intruder – but not before. If nobody comes, she waits for black cat. Black cat attacks; after, her, grey cat. Black cat trots back to the house, purposeful, busy, mission accomplished; grey cat, coward, saunters back, stops to lick her fur, then screams defiance from behind human legs, or a door.

Grey cat, when black cat is occupied with kittens, is almost, not quite, restored to herself. She strolls around the bed at night, choosing her favoured place, not under the sheet now, or on my shoulder, but in the angle behind the knees, or against the curve of the feet. Grey cat licks my face, delicately, looks briefly out of the window at the night, acknowledging tree, moon, stars, winds, or the amours of other cats from which she is now infinitely removed, then settles down. In the morning, when she wishes me to wake, she crouches on my chest and pats my face with her paw. Or, if I am on my side, she crouches looking into my face. Soft, soft touches of her paw. I open my eyes, say I don't want to wake. I close my eyes. Cat gently pats my eyelids. Cat licks my nose. Cat starts purring, two inches from my face. Cat, then, as I lie pretending to be asleep, delicately bites my nose. I laugh and sit up. At which she bounds off my bed and streaks downstairs – to have the back door opened if it is winter, to be fed, if it is summer.

Black cat descends from the top of the house, when she thinks it is time to get up, and sits on the floor looking at me. Sometimes I become conscious of the insistent stare of her yellow eyes. She gets up on to the bed. Grey cat softly growls. But black cat, supported by her nest of kittens, knows her rights and is not afraid. She goes across the foot of the bed, and up the other side, near the wall, ignoring the grey cat. She sits, waiting. Grey cat and black cat exchange long green and yellow stares. Then, if I don't get up, black cat jumps neatly, right over me, and on to the floor. There she looks to see if the gesture has wakened me. If it hasn't, she does it again. And again. Grey cat, then, contemptuous of black cat's lack of subtlety, shows her how things should be done: she crouches to pat my face. Black cat, however, cannot learn the finesse of grey cat: she is impatient of it. She does not know how to pat a face into laughter, or how to bite, gently, mockingly. She knows that if she jumps over me often enough, I will wake up and feed her, and then she can get back to her kittens.

I have watched her trying to copy grey cat. When grey cat lies stretched out for admiration and we say Pretty cat, ppppprrreeetty cat, black cat flops down beside her, in the same position. Grey cat yawns; black cat yawns. Grey cat then pulls herself along under the sofa on her back; and now black cat is defeated, she can't do this trick. So she goes off to her kittens, where, she knows quite well, we come and admire her, too.

Grey cat was turning into a hunter. This was not in pursuit of food. Her hunting is at no time connected with food – that is food considered as a substance to nourish, rather than as a remark, or statement, about her emotions.

One weekend I had forgotten to buy the fresh rabbit which by then was the only thing she would eat. There was tinned catfood. Grey cat, when she is hungry, sits, not in the food corner, black cat's lowly place, but across the kitchen in *her* place. She never miaows for food. She sits near an imaginary saucer, looking at me. If I take no notice, she comes across, weaves about my legs. If I still take no notice, she jumps up, paws on my skirt. Then, she gently nips my calf. As a final comment, she goes to black cat's saucer, turns her back on it, and scratches imaginary dirt over it, saying that as far as she is concerned, it is excrement.

But there *was* no rabbit in the refrigerator. I opened the refrigerator, while she sat close, waiting, then shut it again, in order to say there was nothing in it to interest her, and if she was really hungry, she would have to eat tinned food. She did not understand, and sat herself by the non-existent saucer. I again opened the refrigerator, shut it, indicated the tinned food, and went back to work.

Grey cat then walked out of the kitchen, and in a few minutes came back with two cooked sausages, which she put at my feet.

Wicked cat! Thief of a cat! Amoral cat! Sausage-stealing cat!

At each epithet she closed her eyes in acknowledgment, turned around, scratched imaginary dirt over the sausages, went out of the kitchen, furious.

I ascended to the bedroom, from where I can see the back yards and gardens and walls. Grey cat had come out of the house, and was crossing the garden to the back wall in a lean long hunter's run. She jumped on the back wall, ran along it, disappeared. I could not see where she had gone.

I went back to the kitchen. She appeared with another cooked sausage, which she laid beside the first two. Then, having scratched dirt over that, she left the kitchen and went to sleep on my bed.

Next day, on the kitchen floor, a string of uncooked sausages, and beside them, grey cat, sitting and waiting for me to decipher the implications of this statement.

I thought that perhaps the poor actors from the little theatre were losing their lunches. But no. I watched, from my bedroom window, grey cat trot along the wall, and then jump up and disappear into a house wall at right angles to it. I had noticed that a couple of bricks had been taken out – presumably as ventilation into a kitchen. Not easy for a cat to fit into that small hole, particularly after a three-foot jump from a narrow wall, but that was what she was doing, and still does, when she wishes to convey she is not being suitably fed.

The poor woman in the kitchen, having cooked a couple of sausages for her husband's breakfast, turns and finds them gone. Ghosts! Or she smacks an innocent dog or child. Or she puts out, on a plate, a pound of raw sausages ready for the frying pan. She turns her back for a moment – no sausages. Grey cat is running across our garden, a string of sausages trailing behind her, to deposit them on our kitchen floor. Perhaps this gesture originated in hunting ancestors who were trained to catch and bring food to humans; and the memory of it remains in her brain to be converted into this near-human language.

CHAPTER NINE

In the big sycamore at the bottom of the garden, a thrush builds a nest every year. Every year, the little birds hatch out and take their first flights down into the jaws of waiting cats. Mother bird, father bird, comes down after them, is caught.

The frightened chittering and squealing of a caught bird disturbs the house. Grey cat has brought the bird in, but only to be admired for her skill, for she plays with it, tortures it – and with what grace. Black cat crouches on the stairs and watches. She has never killed a bird. But when, three, four, five hours after grey cat has caught the thing, and it is dead, or nearly so, black cat takes it and tosses it up and about, in emulation of the games grey cat plays. Every summer I rescue birds from grey cat, throw them well away from her, into the air, or into another garden – that is, if not badly damaged, so they may have a chance to recover. When this happens, grey cat is furious, puts her ears back, glares, she does not understand, no, not at all. When she brings a bird in, she is proud. It is, in fact, a present; a fact I did not understand until the summer in Devon. But I scold her and take them away, I am not pleased.

Horrible cat! Bird-torturing cat! Murderous cat! Sadistic cat! Degenerate descendant of honest hunters!

She sparks off anger, in answer to my angry voice; and rushes out of the house with the squealing bird. I lock the back door, shut the windows, while the torture goes on. Later, when everything is quiet, grey cat comes back. She does not wreathe my legs, or greet me. She snubs me, stalks upstairs, and sleeps it off. The corpse of the bird, dead from exhaustion more than from cat's teeth and claws, is stiffening in the garden.

When I had the big tree trimmed, at the request of the neighbours, some of whom dislike it because it shades their gardens, some because 'It makes such a mess everywhere with its leaves,' the tree man stood in the garden and complained. Not directly against me, the customer who after all was going to pay him; but against modern life, which, he says, is anti-tree.

'Every day,' he said, bitter, bitter: 'they ring. I go. There's a fine tree. It's taken a hundred years to grow – what are we, compared to a tree? They say, cut it, its spoiling my roses. Roses! What are roses, compared to a tree? I have to cut a tree for the sake of the roses. Only yesterday I had to cut an ash down to three feet of the ground. To make a table, *she* said, a table, and the tree took a hundred years to grow. She wanted to sit at a table and drink tea and look at her roses. No trees these days, the trees are going. And if you do a good job, they don't like it, no, they want it hacked out of its real shape. And what about the birds? Did you know you had a nest up on that branch?'

'Cats,' I said, 'I'd be pleased if the birds would nest somewhere else.'

'Ah, yes,' said he, 'that's what I hear – the cats. Everybody wants their trees cut, and cats all over the place. What chance for the birds? I tell you, I'm going to give up this job, no one wants an honest craftsman these days – look at those cats, just look at them!'

For the tree man, trees and birds, a unit, a sacred unit to be given preference, I should imagine, over human beings, if he had the decision. As for cats, he'd get rid of them all.

He trimmed, not hacked, the tree; and next spring a

thrush built there, and the little birds came fluttering down as usual. One, however, flew straight into the top back window, the spare room. And spent a day there, so friendly it sat on a chair and looked at me from the distance of a foot, almost eye to eye. It had no impulse of fear towards human beings – not yet. I kept the door shut while grey cat prowled outside. Late that summer's evening, when all the birds were already quiet and asleep, the little bird flew straight back from the window to the tree, without going near the ground. So perhaps it survived.

Which reminds me of a story told me by a lady who lives at the top of a seven-storey block of flats in Paris, near the Place Contrescarpe. She believes in travelling light, having no encumbrances, and being free to move anywhere at any moment. Her husband is a sailor. Well, one afternoon a bird flew in from the treetops and showed no signs of wanting to leave. She is a tidy woman, the last to put up with bird droppings. But 'something got into her'. She put down newspapers and allowed the bird to become friendly. The bird did not leave for the south when winter came, as it should have done; and suddenly my friend understood she was landed with a responsibility. If she threw the bird out now, into wintry Paris, it would die. She had to go on a trip for a couple of weeks. She could not leave the bird. So she bought a cage and took it with her.

Then, she saw herself: 'Imagine it: me! me! arriving at a provincial hotel with a suitcase in one hand, and a bird cage in the other! Me! But what could I do? I had the bird in my room, and that meant I had to be friendly with madame and the maids. I had turned into a lover of humanity – good God! Old ladies stopped me on the stairs. Girls told me about their love problems. I went right back to Paris and sulked until the spring came. Then I threw that bird out of the window with a curse, and ever since then I've kept the windows shut. I simply will *not* be liked and that's that!'

Black cat got pregnant with her second litter when the first were only ten days old. This struck me as uneconomic, but the vet said it was usual. The runt of this litter – and runts are for some reason often the nicest in character, perhaps because they have to make up in charm for what the others have in strength – went to a flat full of students. It was sitting on a shoulder at a third-floor window when a dog barked in the room behind it. On a reflex of fright, it jumped straight out of the window. Everyone rushed down to the pavement to pick up the corpse. But there sat the kitten licking itself. It had not been harmed at all.

Black cat, temporarily kittenless, came downstairs to ordinary life. Probably grey cat had imagined that black cat had removed herself upstairs into responsibility and maternity for good. And so she would have the field to herself. She understood it was not so; she could be threatened at any time. Again the battle for position was fought, and this time it was unpleasant. Black cat had had her kittens, was more sure of herself, and was not so easily intimidated. For instance, she was not going to sleep on the floor or on the sofa.

This matter was settled thus: grey cat slept on the top of the bed, black cat at the foot. But it was grey cat who might wake me. Which act was now performed entirely for the benefit of black cat: the teasing, patting, licking, purring was done while grey cat watched her rival: look, watch me. And the tricks over food: watch me, watch me. And the birds: look what I can do that you can't. I think, during those weeks, the cats were not conscious of humans. They were relating to each other only, like children in rivalry, for whom adults are manoeuvrable, bribable objects, outside the obsession where the children are conscious only of each other. All the world narrows to the other, who must be beaten, outwitted. A small bright, hot and frightful world, like that of fever.

The cats lost their charm. They did the same things, performed the same actions. But charm – lost.

What is charm then? The free giving of a grace, the spending of something given by nature in her role of spendthrift. But there is something uncomfortable here, something intolerable, a grittiness, we are in the presence of injustice. Because some creatures are given so much more than others, they must give it back? Charm is something extra, superfluous, unnecessary, essentially a power thrown away – given. When grey cat rolls on her back in a patch of warm sunlight, luxurious, voluptuous, delightful, that is charm, and it catches the throat. When grey cat rolls, every movement the same, but the eyes narrowed on black cat, it is ugly, and even the movement itself has a hard abrupt quality to it. And black cat watching, or trying to copy something for which she has no natural gift, has an envious furtiveness, as if she were stealing something that does not belong to her. If nature squanders on a creature, as she has done on grey cat, arbitrarily, intelligence and beauty, then grey cat should, in return, squander them as lavishly.

As black cat does her maternity. When she is nested among her kittens, one slender jet paw stretched over them, protective and tyrannical, eyes half-closed, a purr deep in her throat, she is magnificent, generous – and carelessly sure of herself. Meanwhile poor grey cat, denuded of her sex, sits across the room, in her turn envious and grudging, and all her body and her face and her bent back ears saying: I hate her, I hate her.

In short, for a period of some weeks, they were no

74

pleasure to the humans in the house, and surely no pleasure to themselves.

But everything changed suddenly, because there was a trip to the country, where neither had ever been.

CHAPTER TEN

They both had memories of pain and fear associated with the cat basket; so I thought they wouldn't like to travel in it.

They were put loose in the back of the car. Grey cat at once jumped into the front, to my lap. She was miserable. All the way out of London she sat shivering and miaowing, a continuous shrill complaint that drove us all mad. Black cat's plaint was low and mournful, and related to her inner discomfort, not to what was going on around her. Grey cat was shrieking every time a car or lorry appeared in the square of the window. So I put her down at my feet where she could not see the traffic. This did not suit her. She wanted to see what caused the sounds that frightened her. At the same time she hated seeing it. She sat crouched on my knee, lifting her head as a sound increased, saw the black vibrating mass of machinery passing ahead, or falling behind – and miaowed. Experiencing traffic through a cat is a lesson in what we all of us block off every time we get into a car. We do not hear the appalling din – the shaking, the roaring, the screeching. If we did, we would go slightly crazy, like grey cat.

Unable to stand it, we stopped the car, and tried to put her into a basket. She went into a frenzy, hysterical with fear. We let her loose again and tried black cat. She was very happy to be in the basket with the lid shut down over her. For the rest of the journey, black cat crouched in the basket, her black nose through a hole in its side. We stroked her nose and asked how she did; and she replied in the low sad voice, but did not seem unduly upset. Perhaps the fact she was pregnant had something to do with her calm.

Meanwhile grey cat complained. Grey cat miaowed steadily, all the way, six hours of driving, to Devon. Finally she got under the front seat, and the insensate meaningless miaowing went on, and no talking or soothing or comforting had any effect at all. Soon we did not hear it, as we do not hear traffic.

That night was spent in a friend's house in a village. Both cats were put into a large room with a dirt box and food. They could not be let loose because there were cats in the house. Grey cat's terror was forgotten in the need to outdo black cat. She used the dirt box first; ate first; and got on to the only bed. There she sat, defying black cat to get on to it. Black cat ate, used the dirt box, and sat on the floor, looking up at grey cat. When grey cat got off the bed, later, to eat, black cat leaped on the bed and was at once chased off.

So they spent the night. At least, when I woke, there was black cat on the floor, gazing up at grey cat who sat on guard at the bottom of the bed, eyes blazing down.

We moved into a cottage on the moor. It is an old place, which had been empty for some time. There was very little furniture. But it had a large fireplace. These cats had not seen a naked fire. As the logs burned up, grey cat screamed with fright, and fled upstairs and got under a bed, where she stayed.

Black cat sniffed around the downstairs room, discovered the only armchair, and made it her own. She was interested by the fire; was not afraid, as long as she did not go too close.

But she was afraid of the country outside the cottage – fields, grass, trees, not enclosed here in tidy rectangles of brick, but acres of them, cut with low stone walls.

Both cats had to be chased out of the house, for the

purpose of cleanliness, for some days. Then they understood, and took themselves out – briefly, though; not further, at first, than under the windows where there are flowerbeds and cobblestones. Then a bit further, to a stone wall solid with growth. Then into a patch of ground surrounded by walls. And from there, on her first visit, grey cat did not return at once. It was high with nettles, thistles, foxgloves; full of birds and mice. Grey cat crouched at the edge of this little wilderness, whiskers, ears, tail at work – listening and feeling. But she wasn't ready yet to accept her own nature. A bird landing suddenly on a branch was enough to send her scampering back to the house and upstairs under the bed. Where she stayed for some days. But when cars came, with visitors, or people delivering wood, bread, milk, she seemed to feel trapped in the house, and she ran out of it into the fields, where she felt safer. She was, in short, disorientated; she was not anywhere near herself; there was no sense in her instincts. Nor was she eating; it is incredible how long a cat can go without more than a lick of milk or water, when it is disdaining unliked food, or frightened, or a little sick.

We were afraid she might run away – try, perhaps, to get back to London.

When I was about, six, seven, a man sat in our lamp-lit thatched room on the farm one night, caressing a cat. I remember him there stroking the beast, talking to it; and the enclosing circle of lamplight made of them, man and cat, a picture I can see now. I feel again what I felt so strongly then, unease, discomfort. I was standing by my father, and feeling, with him. But what was going on? I prod my memory, try to take it by surprise, to start it working by seeing the warm glow on soft grey fur, hearing again his overemotional voice. But all that comes back is discomfort, wanting him to go. Something was very wrong. Anyway, he wanted the cat. He was a lumberman; he cut timber near the mountains about twenty miles away. At weekends he went back to his wife and children in Salisbury. Now one has to ask: What did he want with a cat in a lumber camp? Why a grown cat and not a kitten, who would learn it belonged to him, or at least, to the camp? Why this cat? Why were we prepared to part with a grown cat, a risky thing, at any time, and to a man only temporarily at the camp, for with the rainy season he would go back to town? Why? Well, the answer of course lies in the tension, the discord in the room that evening.

We made a trip to the camp with the cat.

High among the foothills of a mountain range, park-like country, with large quiet trees. Low among the trees, a nest of white tents in a clearing. The cicadas were shrilling. It was late September or October, because the rains soon broke. Very hot, very dry. Away among the trees, the whine of the saw, steady, monotonous, like the cicadas. Then, an exaggerated silence when it stopped. The crash as another tree fell, and a strong smell of warmed leaves and grass released by the branches crashing down.

We spent the night there in the hot silent place. The cat was left. No telephone at the camp; but the man rang next weekend to say the cat had disappeared. He was sorry; he had put butter on its paws, as my mother had told him, but there was no place to shut it up, because you couldn't shut a cat in a tent; and it had run away.

A fortnight later, in the middle of a hot morning, the cat crept to the house from the bush. She had been a sleek grey cat. Now she was thin, her fur was rough, her eyes wild and frightened. She ran up to my mother and crouched, looking at her, to make sure that this

79

person at least had stayed the same in a frightening world. Then she went up into her arms, purring, crying, in her happiness to be home again.

Well, that was twenty miles, perhaps fifteen as a bird might fly, but not as a cat would have to travel. The cat slipped out of the camp, her nose pointed in the direction her instinct told her she must go. There was no clear road she could take. Between our farm and the camp were a haphazard meander of roads, all of them dirt tracks, and the road to the camp was for four or five miles wheel tracks through dry grass. Unlikely she could follow the car's route back. She must have come straight across country, desolate untenanted veld which had plenty of mice and rats and birds for her to eat, but also cat enemies, like leopards, snakes, birds of prey. She probably moved at night. There were two rivers to get across. They were not large rivers, at the end of the dry season. In places there were stones across; or she might perhaps have examined the banks till she found a place where branches met over the water, and crossed through the trees. She might have swum. I've heard that cats do, though I've never seen it.

The rainy season broke in that two weeks. Both rivers come down in a sudden flood, and unexpectedly. A storm happens upstream, ten, fifteen, twenty miles away. The water banks up, and sweeps down in a wave, anything from two to fifteen feet high. The cat might very easily have been sitting on the edge waiting for a chance to cross the river when the first waters of the season came down. But she was lucky with both rivers. She had got wet through: her fur had been soaked, and had dried. When she had got safely over the second river, there was another ten miles of empty veld. She must have travelled blind, fierce, hungry, desperate, knowing nothing at all except that she must travel, and that she was pointed in the right direction.

Grey cat did not run away, even if she was thinking of it when strangers came to the cottage, and she hid herself in the fields. As for black cat, she made herself at home in the armchair, and stayed there.

For us, it was a time of much hard work, painting walls, cleaning floors, cutting acres of nettles and weeds. We were eating for utility, since there wasn't much time for cooking. And black cat ate with us, happy, since grey cat's fear had removed her as a rival. It was black cat who wreathed our legs when we came in, who purred, who was petted. She sat in the chair, watching us clump in and out of the room in big boots, and regarded the fire, flames, red, always-moving creatures that soon – but not immediately, it took time – persuaded her into the belief of what we take for granted, that a hearth and a cat go together.

Soon she became brave enough to go close to the fire, and sit near it. She ran up on to the pile of logs stacked in the corner, and jumped from there into the old bread oven, which, she decided, would be a better place for kittens than the armchair. But someone forgot, and the oven door was shut. And then, in the middle of a windy night, the mournful cry with which black cat announces helplessness in the face of fate. No complaint of black cat's can be ignored: it is serious, for unlike grey cat, she never complains without good cause. We ran downstairs. The sad miaow came from the wall. Black cat had been locked in the bread oven. Not dangerous; but she was frightened; and she returned to floor-and-arm-chair level, where life was tested and safe.

When grey cat at last decided to come downstairs from her retreat under the bed, black cat was queen of the cottage.

Grey cat attempted to outstare black cat; tried to frighten her off the chair and away from the fire, by tens-ing her muscles threateningly, and making sudden angry movements. Black cat ignored her. Grey cat tried to start the games of precedence over food. But she was unlucky, we were all too busy to play them.

There was black cat, happy in front of the fire, and there was grey cat – well away from it, excluded.

Grey cat sat in the window and miaowed defiance at the moving flames. She came nearer – the fire did not hurt her. And besides, there sat black cat, not much further than whiskers' distance from it. Grey cat came closer, sat on the hearthrug, and watched the flames, ears back, tail twitching. Slowly, she, too, understood that fire behind bars was a benefit. She lay down and rolled in front of it, exposing her creamy belly to the warmth, as she would in sunlight on a London floor. She had come to terms with fire. But not with black cat's taking precedence.

I was alone in the cottage for a few days. Suddenly, there was no black cat. Grey cat sat in the armchair, grey cat was in front of the fire. Black cat was not anywhere in the cottage. Grey cat purred and licked me and bit me; grey cat kept saying how nice it was to be alone, how nice there was no black cat.

I went to look for black cat and found her in a field, hiding. She miaowed sadly, and I took her back to the house, where she ran in terror from grey cat. I smacked grey cat.

Then, when I drove off to shop or to go on the moors, I found black cat coming after me to the car, miaowing. It was not that she wanted to go in the car with me; she did not want me to go at all. I noticed that as I drove away, she climbed on a wall, or into a tree, with her back protected, and she did not come down until I returned. Grey cat was beating her up when I was away. Black cat was by then very pregnant, and this second litter was coming too soon after the first. Grey cat was much stronger than she. This time I smacked grey cat very hard; and I told her what I thought of her. She understood well enough. When I went off driving I put black cat in the cottage, and locked grey cat out. Grey cat sulked. Black cat was subdued; but, supported by us, took back the armchair and would not let grey cat near it.

Grey cat therefore went out in the garden, which was now a half acre of low stubble. She caught some mice and brought them in, leaving them in the middle of the floor. We were not pleased, and threw them out. Grey cat removed herself from the cottage and spent her days in the open.

Down a tiny path between stone walls is a little glade, which, once we had cut the grass that filled it shoulder-high proved to have set in its depths a smooth silent pool. Over the pool hangs a great tree; around it grass, then shrubs and bushes.

There is a stone near the edge of the pool. Grey cat sat on it and looked at the water. Was it dangerous? An expanse of water was as new to her as fire had been. A wind made ripples, which washed at the stone's edge and wetted her paws. She let out a petulant complaint and chased back to the house. Where she sat outside the door, ears moving, looking down the path to the pool. Slowly, she made her way back – not at once: grey cat could never admit so quickly that she might be wrong about something. First she posed herself, licked herself, preened herself, to show her indifference. Then she took a circuitous route to the pool, through the high patch of garden, and down over a rocky bank. The stone was still there, by the water. The water, slightly moving, was there. And over it, the low-hanging tree. Cat picked her way annoyedly through wet grass like an old lady. She sat on the stone and looked at the water. The boughs over her swung and moved in the wind; and again the water washed up to her paws. She withdrew them and sat upright, in a tight close pose. She looked up at the tree, which was in a flurry of movement – *that* was familiar to her. She considered the moving water. Then she did something I've seen her do with her food. Both grey cat and black cat, when offered food that is unfamiliar to them, will put out a paw and touch it. They prod it, pat it, lift the paw to their mouths and first smell, then lick the new substance. Grey cat stretched out a paw to the water, not quite touching it. She withdrew it. She nearly ran away then: her muscles tensed in an impulse of flight, but she decided not. She put down her mouth and licked at the water. But she did not like it. It was not like the water she drinks from my glass beside the bed, at night; nor like the drops that fall from a tap which she puts her mouth sideways to catch. She put a paw right into the water, held it there, brought it out, licked the paw. Water, right enough. Something she knew, or a variety of it.

Grey cat crouched on the stone, face held over the pool, and looked at her reflection. Nothing odd about this: she is familiar with mirrors. But ripples washed back and forth and her reflection disintegrated. She put a paw to her picture in the water, but, unlike a mirror, her paw went through it, into wet. She sat up, obviously annoyed. All too much for her, she stalked daintily back to the house, through the wet grass. There, having told black cat with her eyes how much she hated her, she sat in front of the fire, back to black cat, who watched her, on guard, from the chair.

Grey cat returned to the pool, to the stone. Sitting on the stone, she observed that the tree was a favourite place for birds, who, the moment she left the glade, swooped to the water, drank from it, played in it, flew across it, back and forth. Grey cat now visited the pool for the sake of the birds. But she never caught a bird there. She did not, I think, catch any birds at the cottage. Perhaps because there are so many cats around there and the birds know them?

Driving around the lanes at night, the headlights are always picking up cats; cats in the hedgerows hunting mice, cats trotting along just out of the wheels' reach; cats on gates; cats on walls.

During the first week at the cottage, which is apparently a retreat, well tucked away behind trees and walls from the road and from other houses, several cats came to see who the new people were, and what new cats might have arrived.

In the middle of a night, I saw a reddish tail disappearing out of the open window. I thought, a cat; and went back to sleep. Next day in the shop however, they said foxes came after cats off Dartmoor. All kinds of nasty stories about foxes and cats. But you can't lock cats up in the country; a landscape so full of cats does not seem much evidence of danger from foxes, or from anything else.

The red tail turned out to belong to a handsome reddish-brown cat, which was chased away from the cottage by grey cat, who by now had made the cottage her own. Soon she was chasing away visitors from the gate, which is a hundred yards from the house. The cottage and the fields around it was now grey cat's territory; and we might come across her sunning herself in the long grasses of the little field above the house, or crouched in the long field below it, where there are boggy patches and the birds come to drink.

Then – invasion. The fences on one side were down, and one morning I went to start the fire, and found both cats on the windowsill, temporarily in alliance because outside the window lumbered and crashed and bellowed great smelling beasts which they had never seen before. Black cat let out her sad hollow plaint: Everything is too much, what is this? I can't manage, please help. And grey cat was shrieking defiance from the safety of the sill. The cattle from near fields had broken through the fences and were pouring down past the house to the pool and to the long field which, as it was obvious they knew, was ripe for grazing. There was no one to help me chase the cattle out, not till much later that day; and the farmer did not appear. About fifty beasts made themselves at home, and the cats were distraught. They ran from windowsill to windowsill, and then out of the front door, in short angry rushes, and they complained bitterly, until help appeared and the enormous threatening beasts were shooed back to their own fields. Safety. The cats had learned there was no danger from this sort of animal. For when, a couple of days later, the gate was left open and ponies came in off the moor, the cats did not complain, they were not frightened. Eight little ponies grazed in the old garden; and grey cat picked her way out to them, sat on the stone wall and watched them. She would not come down off the wall; but she was interested, and stayed until they decided to leave.

Cats will watch creatures, activities, actions unfamiliar to them, for hours. The making of a bed, the sweeping of a floor, packing or unpacking a case, sewing, knitting – anything, they will watch. But what are they seeing? A couple of weeks ago, black cat and a couple of kittens sat in the middle of the floor and watched me cut cloth. They observed the moving scissors, the way my hands moved, the way the cloth was put in different heaps. They were there, absorbed, all morning. But I don't suppose they are seeing what we think. What, for instance, does grey cat see when she watches, for half an hour at a time, the way motes move in a column of sunlight? Or when she looks at the leaves moving in the tree outside the window? Or when she lifts her eyes to the moon over the chimney pots?

Black puss, meticulous educator of her kittens, never loses an opportunity for a lesson or a moral. Why should she spend a morning, a kitten on either side, watching the flash of metal in dark cloth, why does she sniff the scissors, sniff the cloth, walk around the field of operations and then communicate some observation to the kittens, so that they perform the same actions – interspersed, since they are kittens, with all kinds of tricks and games? But they sniff the scissors, sniff the cloth, do what their mother has just done. Then sit and watch. She is learning something and teaching them, there is no doubt of it.

CHAPTER ELEVEN

Black cat was not well before her second litter. There was a large bald patch on her back, and she was thin. And she was overanxious: for the week before she did not like being left alone. The cottage was full of people, and it was easy to see she had company. Then, at the weekend, there were three women, and the weather was bad, and we wanted to drive to the coast and watch a cold and stormy sea. But black cat would not let us go. We were all irritable: in tension because we were not going to let her keep more than two kittens, since she was in no state to feed them. That meant we would have to kill some.

On the Sunday she started labour about ten in the morning. It was a slow exhausting business. The first kitten was born about four in the afternoon. She was tired. There was a long interval between the expulsion of the kitten and the reflex when she turned to lick it. It was a fine kitten. But we had agreed not to look too much at the kittens, not to admire these vigorous scraps of life. At last, the second kitten. Now she was very tired, and gave her mournful Please-help-me cry. Right, we said, that's it: she can keep these two and we'll get rid of the rest. We got out a bottle of Scotch and drank a lot of it. Then the third kitten: surely, surely, that was enough? The fourth, the fifth, the sixth. Poor black cat, working hard, expelling kittens, then licking, and cleaning and tidying up – in the depths of the armchair, such activity. At last, she was clean, and the kittens clean and nursing. She lay stretched out, purring and magnificent.

Brave cat, clever cat, beautiful cat . . . but it was no use, we had to get rid of four kittens.

So we did. It was horrible. Then two of us went out into the long field in the dark with torches and we dug a hole while the rain fell steadily, and we buried the four dead kittens and we swore and cursed at nature, at each other, and at life; and then we went back to the long quiet farm room where the fire burned, and there was black cat on a clean blanket, a pretty, proud cat with two kittens – civilization had triumphed again. And we looked incredulously at the kittens, already so strong and standing up side by side on their back paws, their minute pink front paws kneading at their mother's side. Impossible to imagine them dead, but they had been chosen by chance and at random; and if my hand had picked them up an hour ago, descending from above, the hand of fate – then these two would now be lying under heavy wet soil in a rainy field. It was a terrible night; and we drank too much; and decided definitely that we would have black cat operated on, because really, really, it was not worth it.

And grey cat climbed on the arm of the chair, crouched there, and put down a paw to touch a kitten; and black cat lashed out with her paw; and grey cat skulked off out of the house into the rain.

Next day we all felt much better; and drove off to visit the sea, which was blue and calm, the weather having changed during the night.

Black cat's proud purring could be heard all over the big room.

And grey cat brought in several mice, which she laid out on the stone floor. I had realized by then that the mice were part of the one-upmanship, a gift; but it was no use: dead mice are hard to see attractively. As she brought them in, I threw them out; and she looked at me with ears laid back, eyes blazing resentment.

Each morning when I woke up, grey cat was sitting on the bottom of my bed, and on the floor a newly killed mouse.

Oh kind cat. Clever cat. Thank you so much, cat. But I threw them out. And black cat went after them and ate them.

I was sitting on the stone wall of the garden when I saw grey cat hunting.

It was a day of thin fast-moving cloud, so that across fields, cottage, trees, and the garden fled sunlight and dark; and grey cat was a shadow among the shadows under a lilac tree. She was very still; but looking closely, you could see faint movement in her whiskers and ears; so she was no stiller than was natural where leaves and grass shivered in a light wind. She was looking, eyes shifting, at stubble a few feet off. As I watched, she moved forward in a low fast crouch, as a shadow moves under a swaying branch. There were three little mice creeping about in a litter of drying grass. They had not seen her. They stopped to nibble, moved on, sat up again to look about. Why, then, did not cat pounce at once? She was not four feet from them. I stayed there; cat stayed there; the mice went on with their lives. Half an hour passed. The tip of cat's tail moved: not impatiently; but the visible expression of her thought: There's plenty of time. A dazzling cloud with the mid-day sun behind it shed a couple of dozen fat drops, each one gold. A drop fell on cat's face. She looked annoyed, but did not move. The golden drops splashed among the mice. They froze, then sat up, and looked. I could see the tiny black eyes looking. A couple of drops fell on cat's head. She shook it. The mice froze, and cat pounced, a grey streak. A small miserable squeaking. Cat sat up with a mouse in her mouth. It was wriggling. Cat dropped the mouse; it crept a little way; she was after it. Out darted a paw; with all her wicked claws extended, she made a scooping movement inwards, bringing the mouse towards her. It squeaked. She bit. The squeaking stopped. She sat licking herself, delicately. Then she picked up the mouse and trotted across to me, throwing it up in her mouth and catching it exactly as she had done with her kittens. She laid it at my feet. She had seen me there all the time: had given no sign of it.

People went away from the cottage, and I was alone. There was more time for petting and talking to the cats.

One day in the kitchen I was cutting up their food in the saucers on the table when grey cat leaped up and began eating from one of them. Black cat waited on the floor. But when I put down the two saucers, grey cat walked away: she was not going to eat off the floor.

Next day, the same. Grey cat was trying to make me feed her on the table, a superior place, while black cat stayed on the floor to eat. I said to her, No; it was absurd; and for three days she ate nothing from the house; though perhaps she ate mice. Certainly not when she could be seen, however. On the fourth day she leaped up as usual to the table, and I thought: Well then, it's interesting, let's see. She was pleased to eat all there was in the saucer; and all the time she was glancing down at black cat who was eating on the floor: Look at me, I'm favoured.

In a few days, black cat leaped on the table, trying to get the same privilege. At which grey cat, ears back, got on to the windowsill above the table, and waited for me to put the saucer up there for her. If black cat had achieved the status of the table, she decided, then she was going to demand one better.

At which I lost my temper, and told the pair of them they were a nuisance, and they would eat on the floor or not at all.

Grey cat then went off out of the house and ate and

drank nothing for some days. She was out of the house all day; then day and all night – she was away two, three days at a time. It is at this point, on the farm in Africa, that we would have said: Grey cat is going wild. And we would have taken steps, fussed over her, locked her up, reminded her of her domestic nature. But probably, in highly populated England, going wild is not so easy. Even on Dartmoor there must always be the lights of a house gleaming somewhere not too far off.

Next time she came back, I gave in; and fed her on the table, and praised her; and snubbed black cat just a little – after all, she did have her kittens. And grey cat came back into the house, and settled at nights on the foot of my bed. And when she brought in mice, I made a short flattering speech over each one.

Black cat ate the dead mice. Grey cat never did. It was interesting that black cat did not start eating a mouse until I had seen it. Once a corpse had been accepted by me, and grey cat praised, then black cat got down off the chair, and ate it, tidily, methodically, while grey cat watched, and made no attempt to stop her. Though she did try putting them on a table, a window-sill, where it seemed she hoped black cat would not see them. Black cat always did: always climbed up and ate the mouse.

Then, one morning, something extraordinary happened.

I had gone shopping in Okehampton. I came back and saw, in the middle of the floor, a little cairn or mound of greenery. Grey cat sat near to it, watching me. Black cat was waiting with her kittens in the armchair. They both wanted me to pay attention to the green mound.

I went to look. Under the green stuff, a dead mouse. Grey cat had caught the mouse, and had put it on the floor as a present. But I had been longer coming back than she expected; and so she had had time for decoration – or perhaps it was a warning to black cat: leave the mouse alone.

She must have made three journeys to the hedge, which was freshly sickled, to carry in three sprays of wild geranium, which she had placed carefully over the mouse.

As I complimented her, she never took her eyes off black cat – a nasty, superior, triumphant look.

I've been told since that lions sometimes drag branches over a fresh kill. To mark it? To protect it from jackals and hyenas? To shade it from the sun?

Had grey cat remembered, through thousands of years, her kinship with the lion?

But I do wonder: suppose black cat had never come to live in our house, suppose grey cat had remained sole owner of us, and the places we live in, would she, as she settled into middle age, have bothered to charm and cajole? Would she have developed this complicated language of self-esteem and vanity? Would she have ever caught a bird or a mouse? I think very likely not.

CHAPTER TWELVE

Time to return to London. Grey cat was loose in the back of the car, and again monotonously complained, all six hours of the journey. A short silence, as she dozed off. Then, a particularly loud miaow when she woke and realized she was still suffering.

And the phenomenon so noticeable on the way down: it was not enough to experience noise, movement, discomfort; she wanted to *see* the terrifying loomings-up, the fallings-away, of other vehicles. I swear there was a satisfaction in her miaow then. Like a neurotic person, she was getting pleasure from it.

Black cat sat quiet in the basket with her two kittens, fed them, purred when I put a finger through to stroke her nose; and did not complain unless grey cat's voice rose particularly high, when she joined in for a few moments, matching miaow for miaow. It sounded as if she were thinking: if *she* is doing it, then I suppose it's the right thing to do. But she couldn't keep it up.

I released the two animals inside the house, and at once they were at home. Black cat took her two kittens to the bathroom, where she likes to have them in the fortnight they are the right age to be taught. Grey cat at once went upstairs, and took possession of the bed.

Autumn. The back doors shut because of the heating; dirt boxes brought in to the verandah; cats let out when they ask to be. Not very often: they seem happy enough with an indoors existence while it is cold.

Black cat went rampageously on heat. She came on heat the usual ten days after the birth of the kittens, in Devon. It was while the grey cat was away hunting.

Black cat left the kittens in the chair in front of the fire, and went out to look for a male cat. But for some reason there were none around: probably grey cat had chased them away too thoroughly. But none came running to black cat, as they come running across gardens and walls in London when she calls to them. She would have to go further afield. She took the kittens upstairs where she felt they would be safe, and went up to the gate where she sat calling and yowling. She rushed back briefly to the kittens, since for black cat not even sex can take precedence over motherhood; fed them, went off again. She ate hardly at all, and yowled and yearned her way into a gaunt and bony condition. When I woke in the night I heard her calling up near the gate. But she did not find a mate; and she had got fat and sleek again.

In the couple of months since we left London, the cat population had changed. There was not one of the original cats left. Grey tabby had gone; and the long-haired black-and-white cat had gone. The comparative newcomer, the white cat with grey patches, remained. No other cats around for that mating; so the patched white cat became the father, and we were interested to see what dice the genes would throw this time.

The autumn was cold and wet. When I went out to the back, grey cat, black cat came too, and walked fussily over wet leaves, and chased each other back to the house. A sort of friendship was beginning. They have never yet licked each other, or slept close. But they were beginning to play a little; though more often than not the one who started play would be snubbed in a hiss. They always meet with caution, sniff each other's noses – is that you, friend or foe? It is like the handshake of enemies.

Black cat grew heavy, and slept a great deal. Grey

cat was boss cat again, did her tricks, displayed herself.

Black cat again had her kittens in the top room, and we let her keep all six of them. We were still too sore after the murder of the last lot to go through it again.

When they were mobile, black cat decided there was only one thing she wanted, only one thing, and she was going to have it: the kittens must be under my bed. This was because the room upstairs was, much to her annoyance, not occupied all the time, so she could have company and admiration. The studying girl was having a gay and social Christmas. Black cat is a sticker. She brought the kittens down. I took them downstairs to the bathroom, in skirtfuls. Black cat brought them back. I took them down. She brought them back. Finally brute force won: I simply locked the door.

This is the time when, kittens at their most enchanting, one longs for them to leave. Kittens underfoot everywhere, kittens on tables, chairs, windowsills, kittens tearing the furniture to pieces. Everywhere you looked, a black charmer – because they were all black, six black kittens, and the whitey-grey father had had no effect on their looks at all.

And among them, black cat, indefatigable, devoted, dutiful, watching them every moment. She was drinking pints and pints of milk more than she wanted, because every time a kitten was near, she had to teach it how to drink. She ate every time a kitten was near a saucer. I've seen black cat, obviously disinclined for even one more mouthful of food, stop as a kitten went out of a room, lick herself, prepare to rest. That kitten or another came in. Black cat bent over the saucer, and ate, with the low trilling sound she uses for coaxing her kittens. Kitten came, sat curiously by the mother, watching her eat. Cat ate on, slower, forcing herself to eat. Kitten sniffed at the food, decided warm milk was best, went to black cat's nipples. Black cat made a low commanding sound. Kitten, obedient, went to the saucer and made a small lick or two; then, having done as ordered, raced back to black cat who flopped over on her side to nurse.

Or black cat at the dirt box. She has been out in the garden; has just emptied herself. But a kitten is due a lesson. Black cat gets on to the dirt box in the appropriate position. She calls to the kittens: look at me. She sits on, while the kittens stroll around, watching or not watching. When she knows one has understood, she gets off the box and sits by it, encouraging the kitten with purrs and calls to do as it has been shown. Minute black kitten copies mamma. Success! Kitten looks surprised. Mamma licks kitten.

Black cat's kittens never go through a period of messing. Indeed, like obsessively trained children, they are overanxious about the whole business. Caught playing some way from the dirt box, a kitten will send out a wild mew; will go through the motions of getting into the right position—but again a desperate mew; it is not in the right place. Black cat comes running to the rescue; black cat urges kitten into the room where the dirt box is. Kitten runs to it, leaking a little perhaps, mewing. On the dirt box, what relief, while mother sits by, approving. Oh what a good clean kitten I am, says kitten's pose and face. Kitten gets off the box, and is licked in approval, the random carelessly confident lick that is like a kiss.

This kitten is all right; but what about the others? Off goes black cat, busy, busy, to check on faces, tails, fur. And — where are they? At the age just before they leave, they are all over the house. Black cat, frantic, rushes about, up and down stairs and in and out of rooms; where are you, where are you? The kittens curl themselves up in bunches, behind boxes, in cupboards. They don't come out when she calls to them. So she flops down near them, and lies on guard, eyes half-closed for possible enemies or intruders.

She wears herself out. The kittens leave, one after another. She does not seem to notice until there are two left. She watches over them, anxious. Then there is one kitten. Black cat devotes all that ferocious maternity to one kitten. The last one goes. And black cat rushes all over the house, looking for it, miaowing. Then, a switch is turned somewhere – black cat has forgotten what is upsetting her. She climbs up the stairs and goes to sleep on the sofa, her place. She might never have had kittens.

Until the next lot. Kittens, kittens, showers of kittens, visitations of kittens. So many, you see them as Kitten, like leaves growing on a bare branch, staying heavy and green, then falling, exactly the same every year. People coming to visit say: What happened to that lovely kitten? What lovely kitten? They are all lovely kittens.

Kitten. A tiny lively creature in its transparent membrane, surrounded by the muck of its birth. Ten minutes later, damp but clean, already at the nipple. Ten days later, a minute scrap with soft hazy eyes, its mouth opening in a hiss of brave defiance at the enormous menace sensed bending over it. At this point, in the wild, it would confirm wildness, become wild cat. But no, a human hand touches it, the human smell envelops it, a human voice reassures it. Soon it gets out of its nest, confident that the gigantic creatures all around will do it no harm. It totters, then strolls, then runs all over the house. It squats in its earth box, licks itself, sips milk, then tackles a rabbit bone, defends it against the rest of the litter. Enchanting kitten, pretty kitten, beautiful furry babyish delicious little beast – then off it goes. And its personality will be formed by the new household, the new owner, for while it is with its mother, it is just kitten – though, since it is the child of black cat, a very well-brought-up kitten indeed.

Perhaps, like grey cat, the poor old spinster cat, black cat when we eventually have her 'doctored' will look at kittens as if she does not know what they are. Perhaps her memory won't give up the knowledge of kittens, though while she has them her days, her nights, her every instinct is for them, and she would die any death for them, if it were necessary.

There was a she-cat, all those years ago. I don't remember why it went wild. Some awful battle must have been fought, beneath the attention of the humans. Perhaps some snub was administered, too much for cat pride to bear. This old cat went away from the house for months. She was not a pretty beast, an old ragbag patched and streaked in black and white and grey and fox-colour. One day she came back and sat at the edge of the clearing where the house was, looking at the house, the people, the door, the other cats, the chickens – the family scene from which she was excluded. Then she crept back into the bush. Next evening, a silent golden evening, there was the old cat. The chickens were being shooed into the runs for the night. We said, perhaps she is after the chickens, and shouted at her. She flattened herself into the grass and disappeared. Next evening, there she was again. My mother went down to the edge of the bush and called to her. But she was wary, would not come close. She was very pregnant: a large gaunt beast, skin over prominent bones, dragging the heavy lump of her belly. She was hungry. It was a dry year. The long dry season had flattened and thinned the grass, cauterized bushes: everything in sight was skeleton, dry sticks of grass; and the tiny leaves fluttering on them, merely shadows. The bushes were twig; trees, their load of leaf thinned and dry, showed the plan of their trunk and branches. The veld was all bones. And the hill our house was on, in the wet season so tall and lush and soft and thick, was stark. Its shape, a low

99

swelling to a high ridge, then an abrupt fall into a valley, showed beneath a stiff fringe of stick and branch. The birds, the rodents, had perhaps moved away to lusher spots. And the cat was not wild enough to move after them, away from the place she still thought of as home. Perhaps she was too worn by hunger and her load of kittens to travel.

We took down milk, and she drank it, but carefully, her muscles tensed all the time for flight. Other cats from the house came down to stare at the outlaw. When she had drunk the milk, she ran away back to the place she was using to hide in. Every evening she came to the homestead to be fed. One of us kept the other resentful cats away; another brought milk and food. We kept guard till she had eaten. But she was nervous: she snatched every mouthful as if she were stealing it; she kept leaving the plate, the saucer, then coming back. She ran off before the food was finished; and she would not let herself be stroked, would not come close.

One evening we followed her, at a distance. She disappeared halfway down the hill. It was land that had at some point been trenched and mined for gold by a prospector. Some of the trenches had fallen in – heavy rains had washed in soil. The shafts were deserted, perhaps had a couple of feet of rain water in them. Old branches had been dragged across to stop cattle falling in. In one of these holes, the old cat must be hiding. We called her, but she did not come, so we left her.

The rainy season broke in a great dramatic storm, all winds and lightning and thunder and pouring rain. Sometimes the first storm can be all there is for days, even weeks. But that year we had a couple of weeks of continuous storms. The new grass sprang up. The bushes, trees, put on green flesh. Everything was hot and wet and teeming. The old cat came up to the house once or twice; then did not come. We said she was catching mice again. Then, one night of heavy storm, the dogs were barking, and we heard a cat crying just outside the house. We went out, holding up storm lanterns into a scene of whipping boughs, furiously shaking grass, rain driving past in grey curtains. Under the verandah were the dogs, and they were barking at the old cat, who crouched out in the rain, her eyes green in the lantern-light. She had had her kittens. She was just an old skeleton of a cat. We brought out milk for her, and chased away the dogs, but that was not what she wanted. She sat with the rain whipping over her, crying. She wanted help. We put raincoats on over our night-clothes and sloshed after her through a black storm, with the thunder rolling overhead, lightning illuminating sheets of rain. At the edge of the bush we stopped and peered in – in front of us was the area where the old trenches were, the old shafts. It was dangerous to go plunging about in the undergrowth. But the cat was in front of us, crying, commanding. We went carefully with storm lanterns, through waist high grass and bushes, in the thick pelt of the rain. Then the cat was not to be seen, she was crying from somewhere beneath our feet. Just in front of us was a pile of old branches. That meant we were on the edge of a shaft. Cat was somewhere down it. Well, we were not going to pull a small mountain of slippery dead branches off a crumbling shaft in the middle of the night. We flashed the light through interstices of the branches, and we thought we saw the cat moving, but were not sure. So we went back to the house, leaving the poor beasts, and drank cocoa in a warm lamplit room, and shivered ourselves dry and warm.

But we slept badly, thinking of the poor cat, and got up at five with the first light. The storm had gone over, but everything was dripping. We went out into a cool dawnlight, and red streaks showed in the east where the sun would come up. Down we went into the soaked bush, to the pile of old branches. Not a sign of the cat.

This was a shaft about eighty feet deep, and it had been cross-cut twice, at about ten feet, and then again much deeper. We decided the cat must have put her kittens into the first cut, which ran for about twenty feet, downwards at a slant. It was hard to lift off those heavy wet branches: it took a long time. When the mouth of the shaft was exposed, it was not the clean square shape it had been. The earth had crumbled in, and some light branches and twigs from the covering heap had sunk, making a rough platform about fifteen feet down. On to this had been washed and blown earth and small stones. So it was like a thin floor – but very thin: through it we could see the gleam of rain water from the bottom of the shaft. A short way down, not very far now that the mouth of the shaft had sunk, at about six feet, we could see the opening of the cross-cut, a hole about four feet square, now that it, too, had crumbled. Lying face down on the slippery red mud, holding on to bushes for safety, you could see a good way into the cut – a couple of yards. And there was the cat's head, just visible. It was quite still, sticking out of the red earth. We thought the cut had fallen in with all that rain, and she was half buried, and probably dead. We called her: there was a faint rough sound, then another. So she wasn't dead. Our problem then was, how to get to her. Useless to fix a windlass on to that soaked earth which might landslide in at any moment. And no human could put weight on to that precarious platform of twigs and earth: hard to believe it had been able to take the weight of the cat, who must have been jumping down to it several times a day.

We tied a thick rope to a tree, with big knots in it at three-foot intervals, and let it down over the edge, trying not to get it muddied and slippery. Then one of us went down on the rope with a basket, until it was possible to reach into the cut. There was the cat, crouched against the soaked red soil – she was stiff with cold and wet. And beside her were half a dozen kittens, about a week old and still blind. Her trouble was that the storms of that fortnight had blown so much rain into the cut that the sides and roof had partly fallen in; and the lair she had found, which had seemed so safe and dry, had become a wet crumbling death trap. She had come up to the house so that we could rescue the kittens. She had been frightened to come near the house because of the hostility of the other cats and the dogs, perhaps because she now feared us, but she had overcome her fear to get help for the kittens. But she had not been given help. She must have lost all hope that night, as the rain lashed down, as earth slid in all around her, as the water crept up behind her in the dark collapsing tunnel. But she had fed the kittens, and they were alive. They hissed and·spat as they were lifted into the basket. The cat was too stiff and cold to get out by herself. First the angry kittens were taken up, while she crouched in the wet earth waiting. The basket descended again, and she was lifted into it. The family were taken up to the house, where she was given a corner, food, protection. The kittens grew up and found homes; and she stayed a house cat – and presumably went on having kittens.

CHAPTER THIRTEEN

Spring. The doors open. The earth smells new. Grey cat and black cat chase and scamper all over the garden, and up on to the walls. They loll in weak sunlight – but well away from each other. They get up from rolling, and meet, cautiously, in a sniff nose to nose, this side, then that. Black cat goes indoors to the duties of maternity; grey cat is off, hunting.

Grey cat has brought back new habits from Devon. Her hunting is swifter, deadlier, more sensitive. She will lie flat along a wall, watching the tree for hours, not moving at all. Then, when the bird flies down, she pounces. Or, surprisingly, she doesn't pounce. There is the flat roof of the theatre which overlooks the neighbour's patch of garden, where birds like to come. Grey cat lies on the roof, not crouched, but stretched out, chin on her paw, her tail still. And she is not asleep. Her eyes are intent on the starlings, the thrushes, the sparrows. She watches. Then she gets up; her back arches, slowly; she stretches her back legs, her front legs. The birds freeze, seeing her there. But she yawns, then ignores them, and delicately picks her way along the wall and into the house. Or she sits on the bottom of my bed and watches them through the window. Perhaps her tail twitches slightly – but that is all. She can be there half an hour, an indifferent observer: or so it seems. Then, in a moment, something will spring the hunter's instinct. She sniffs, her whiskers move: then she's off the bed, and down the stairs and into the garden. There she creeps, deadly beast, under the wall. She quietly leaps up the wall – but not on it, no: grey cat, like a cat in a cartoon, hooks her front paws on to the wall, puts her chin on the wall, supports her weight on her back legs, surveys the state of affairs in the next garden. She is very funny. You have to laugh. But why? For once grey cat is not posing, is unconscious of herself, is not arranging herself for admiration and comment. Perhaps it is the contrast between her absolute intensity, her concentration, and the uselessness of what she is going to do: kill a small creature which she doesn't even want to eat.

While you are still laughing, she's up and over the wall, has caught a bird, and is back on the wall with it. She is running back into the house with the bird – but no, the inexplicable human beings have rushed downstairs to shut the back door. So she plays with the bird in the garden until she tires of the game.

Once a bird swooped down past a roof, saw the jut of a wall too late, crashed into it, and lay stunned, or dead, on the earth. I was in the garden with grey cat. We went together to the bird. Grey cat was not very interested – a dead bird, she seemed to think. I remember how black cat revived with hands' warmth, and held the bird enclosed in my hand. I sat on the edge of a flowerbed; grey cat sat near, watching. I held the bird between us. It stirred, trembled; its head lifted, its eyes unfilmed. I was watching cat. She did not respond. The bird put its cold claws down against my palm, and pushed, like a baby trying out its strength with its feet. I let the bird sit on one palm, covered with the other. It seemed full of life. All this time grey cat merely watched. Then I lifted the bird on my palm, where it sat for a moment. Still cat did not respond. Then the bird lifted its wings and sped off into the air. At that last moment cat's hunting instincts were touched, her muscles obeyed, she gathered herself for a spring. But by then the bird was off and gone, so she relaxed and licked herself. Her movements during this incident had the same quality as those made before she had her first litter – when she was prompted briefly and inconclusively to make a lair for the kittens. Certain actions were made; part of her was involved; but she did not really know about it; she was not set in action as a whole creature.

Perhaps it is some definite movement a bird makes, some particular signal, that attracts the hunter in a cat, and until that movement occurs, a cat is not involved with the bird, has no relation to it. Or perhaps it is a sound. I am sure the frenzied chittering of a caught bird, the squeaking of a mouse, arouses a cat's desire to torture and torment. After all, even in a human, the frightened sound arouses strong emotions: panic, anger, disapproval – the springs of morality are touched. You want to rescue the creature, beat the cat, or shut the whole beastly business out where you can't see or hear it, don't have to know about it. A tiny turn of the screw, and you'd be sinking your jaws in, ripping claws through soft flesh.

But what screw? That's the point.

Perhaps for a cat it isn't sound, but something else.

That great South African naturalist, Eugene Marais, describes in his remarkable and beautiful book, *The Soul of the White Ant,* how he tried to find out how a certain kind of beetle communicates. It was a *toktokkie* beetle. It is not equipped with auditory organs; yet everyone brought up on the veld knows its system of small knocking sounds. He describes how he spent weeks with the beetle, watching it, thinking about it, making experiments. And then, suddenly, that marvellous moment of insight when he came to the until then not obvious conclusion that it was not sound, but a vibration which the beetle was using: a vibration so subtle it is out of our range completely. And the symphony of clickings, squeakings, chirpings, buzzings, which is how we experience the insect world – on a hot night, for instance – is for them signals of a different kind, which we are too crude to catch. Well yes, of course: obvious. As soon as you see it, that is.

Under our noses, all these complicated languages which we don't know how to interpret.

You can watch a thing a dozen times, thinking, How charming, or how strange, until, and always unexpectedly, sense is suddenly made.

For instance: when black cat's kittens are at the walking stage, grey cat will always, at a certain point, but never when black cat is watching, creep up to a kitten – and this is what is so odd – as if kittens are a new phenomenon, as if she has never had kittens herself. She creeps *behind,* or *sideways,* to the kitten. She will sniff at it, or put a paw to it, tentative, experimental: she might even give it a hasty lick or two. But not from the front. Not once have I seen her approaching from the front. If the kitten turns and faces her, perhaps even in friendly curiosity, not hostile at all, grey cat spits, backs, her fur goes up – she is warned off by some mechanism.

I thought this was just grey cat, whose sexual and maternal instincts have been taken from her, and who is such a coward. But a fortnight ago, a five-week-old kitten was taking its first walk in the garden: sniffing, looking, adventuring. Its father, the whitish cat, came up; and in exactly the same way as grey cat, in a creeping cautious way. It sniffed at the kitten from behind. The kitten turned around and faced this new creature, and at once the big male cat backed away, hissing and frightened, *threatened* by this minute thing which it could have killed with one snap of its jaws.

Nature protecting a tiny creature from an adult of its own species during the period it can't fight for itself through strength?

CHAPTER FOURTEEN

The cats are now four years old, two years old.

Grey cat is less than halfway through her life – if she has luck.

Not long ago, she wasn't in when we went to bed. She didn't come in that night at all. Next day, no grey cat. That night, since grey cat was not in the prestige position, black cat took it.

The day after that I switched on all the defence mechanisms: well, it's only a cat, etc. And did the routine things: Has anyone seen a Siamese-shaped grey cat with a cream underside and black markings? No one had.

Very well then, when black cat had her next litter, we would keep one, and at least we would have two cats in the house who were friends, who would enjoy each other.

When she had been gone four days, grey cat came back, she came running along the walls. Perhaps she had been stolen and had escaped; perhaps she had been visiting some family who admired her.

Black cat was not pleased to see her.

From time to time people in the house lecture the cats, when they think no one is listening: Fools, idiots, why can't you be friends? Just think what fun you are missing, think how nice it would be!

Last week I trod on grey cat's tail by mistake: she let out a squawk, and black cat leaped in for a kill: instant reflex. Grey cat had lost favour and protection, so black cat thought, and this was her moment.

I apologized to grey cat, petted them both. They

accepted these attentions, watching each other all the time, and went their separate ways to their separate saucers, their separate sleeping places. Grey cat rolls on the bed, yawns, preens, purrs: favourite cat, boss cat, queen cat by right of strength and beauty.

Black cat tends to settle these days – there are no kittens around for the moment – in a corner of the hallway where she has her back to the wall, and can check on invaders from the garden, and watch grey cat's movements up and down the stairs.

When she dozes off, eyes half-closed, she becomes what she really is, her real self when not tugged into fussy devotion by motherhood. A small sleek, solid little animal, she sits, a black, black cat with her noble, curved, aloof profile.

'Cat from the Shades! Plutonic cat! Cat for an alchemist! Midnight cat!'

But black cat is not interested in compliments today, she does not want to be bothered. I stroke her back; it arches slightly. She lets out half a purr, in polite acknowledgment to the alien, then gazes ahead into the hidden world behind her yellow eyes.

THE WORLD'S GREATEST NOVELISTS NOW AVAILABLE IN GRANADA PAPERBACKS

Doris Lessing

Novels

The Grass is Singing	£1.50 ☐
The Golden Notebook	£2.50 ☐
Briefing for a Descent into Hell	£1.95 ☐

'Children of Violence' Series

Martha Quest	£1.50 ☐
A Proper Marriage	£1.50 ☐
A Ripple from the Storm	£1.50 ☐
Landlocked	£1.25 ☐
The Four-Gated City	£2.50 ☐

'Canopus in Argos: Archives'

Shikasta	£1.95 ☐
The Marriages Between Zones Three, Four, and Five	£1.95 ☐
The Sirian Experiments (*forthcoming*)	£1.95 ☐

Non-Fiction

In Pursuit of the English (*Autobiography*)	£1.50 ☐
Particularly Cats	95p ☐
Going Home	95p ☐

All these books are available to your local bookshop or newsagent, or can be ordered direct from the publisher. Just tick the titles you want and fill in the form below.

Name ....

Address ....

....

Write to Granada Cash Sales, PO Box 11, Falmouth, Cornwall TR10 9EN

Please enclose remittance to the value of the cover price plus:

UK: 40p for the first book, 18p for the second book plus 13p per copy for each additional book ordered to a maximum charge of £1.49.

BFPO and EIRE: 40p for the first book, 18p for the second book plus 13p per copy for the next 7 books, thereafter 7p per book.

OVERSEAS: 60p for the first book and 18p for each additional book.

Granada Publishing reserve the right to show new retail prices on covers, which may differ from those previously advertised in the text or elsewhere.

GF181